BUMPER INSTANT ART

MAKE AND DO

Kevin Mayhew

First published in 2001 by
KEVIN MAYHEW LTD
Buxhall, Stowmarket, Suffolk IP14 3BW
E-mail: info@kevinmayhewltd.com

Bumper Instant Art Make and Do is a compilation of material previously published in *Instant Art for Bible Action Models, Instant Art for Pre-school Make and Do,* and *Instant Art Make and Do.*

9 8 7 6 5 4 3 2 1 0

ISBN 1 84003 769 5
Catalogue No 1396086

Cover design by Jonathan Stroulger
Printed and bound in Great Britain

Contents

Old Testament

Days of creation spinner	Genesis 1:1-31, 2:1-3	1
God's creation – Days 3 and 4	Genesis 1	2
Noah's animals	Genesis 6-8	3
Abraham	Genesis 12-13	4
Isaac and Rebekah	Genesis 24	5
Jacob and Esau	Genesis 27	6
Joseph and his brothers	Genesis 37	7
Moses: baby in a basket	Exodus 2:1-10	8
Moses: God's call and signs	Exodus 3-4	9
Moses: plagues of Egypt spinner	Exodus 5-12	10
Moses crosses the Red Sea	Exodus 13-14	12
Joshua marches round Jericho	Joshua 6	13
God calls Samuel	1 Samuel 1-3	14
Samuel anoints Saul	1 Samuel 8-10	15
David and Goliath	1 Samuel 17	16
Elijah and the prophets of Baal	1 Kings 18	17
Naaman the leper	2 Kings 5	18
Nehemiah rebuilds Jerusalem	Nehemiah 1-6	19
The fiery furnace	Daniel 3	20
Belshazzar's banquet	Daniel 5	21
Daniel in the lions' den	Daniel 6	22
Jonah and the whale	Jonah 1-3	23

New Testament

John the Baptist	Matthew 3:1-11	24
Follow me!	Matthew 4:12-23	26
Jesus' parables – The precious pearl	Matthew 13:45-46	28
Matthew the tax collector	Matthew 9:9-13	30
Priceless Treasure	Matthew 13:44-46	32
Have faith	Matthew 14:22-33	34
Be forgiving	Matthew 18:23-35	36
Palm Sunday	Matthew 21:1-11	38
Be ready	Matthew 25:1-13	40
Gifts from God	Matthew 25:14-30	42
The shepherd and his flock	Mark 6:30-34	44
The camel and the needle	Mark 10:17-25	46
The generous woman	Mark 12:41-44	48
Jesus is born	Luke 2:1-20	50

Jesus heals the lame man	Luke 5:18-25	52
Jesus heals the centurion's servant	Luke 7:1-10	53
Good fruit	Luke 6:43-45	54
The precious perfume	Luke 7:36-50	56
Jesus heals Jairus' daughter	Luke 8:40-56	57
Make time to listen	Luke 10:38-42	58
Jesus' parables – The wedding feast	Luke 14:15-24	60
Jesus' parables – The lost sheep	Luke 15:4-6	61
Always be honest	Luke 16:10-11	62
Thank you, Jesus	Luke 17:12-19	64
Jesus heals the ten lepers	Luke 17:11-19	66
Jesus and Zacchaeus	Luke 19:1-10	67
The story of Zacchaeus	Luke 19:1-10	68
Jesus is risen	Luke 24:1-10	70
Jesus turns water into wine	John 2:1-11	71
Jesus feeds the people	John 6:1-15	72
Jesus feeds 5000 people	John 6:1-15	74
Jesus heals the blind man	John 9	75
A grain of wheat	John 12:23-27	76
I will not leave you on your own	John 14:16-20	78
Jesus before Pontius Pilate	John 18:33-37	80
Jesus is alive. Alleluia! Alleluia!	John 20:1-9	82
Doubting Thomas	John 20:19-29	84
Jesus ascends to heaven	Acts 1:1-10	86
The coming of the Holy Spirit	Acts 2:1-21	87
Peter and John and the lame man	Acts 3:7-10	88
Philip and the Ethiopian	Acts 8:26-40	90
Eutychus	Acts 20:6-12	91
Paul's shipwreck	Acts 27	92

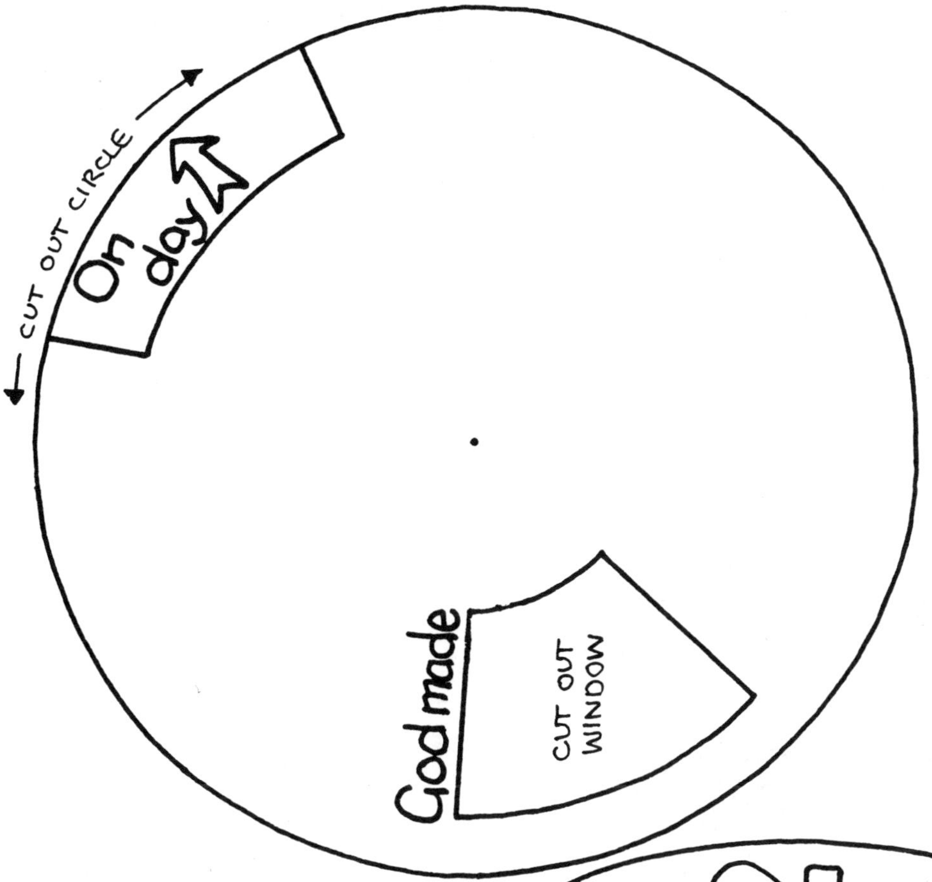

1. Photocopy onto thin card.
2. Colour in numbers and pictures.
3. Cut out both circles.
4. Cut window in smaller circle.
5. Pierce centres of circles.
6. Placing smaller circle on top, put paper fastener through centre of both circles.
7. Turn lower circle to see correct picture in window – see diagram.

1. Photocopy onto thin card.
2. Colour in. On circle, colour sky around sun light blue gradually darkening to dark sky around moon. Cut out.
3. Fold outwards on dotted line.
4. Pierce dots A, B and C with piece folded so C is in line with A.
5. Attach paper fastener through A, then B, then C.

Turn to change day to night

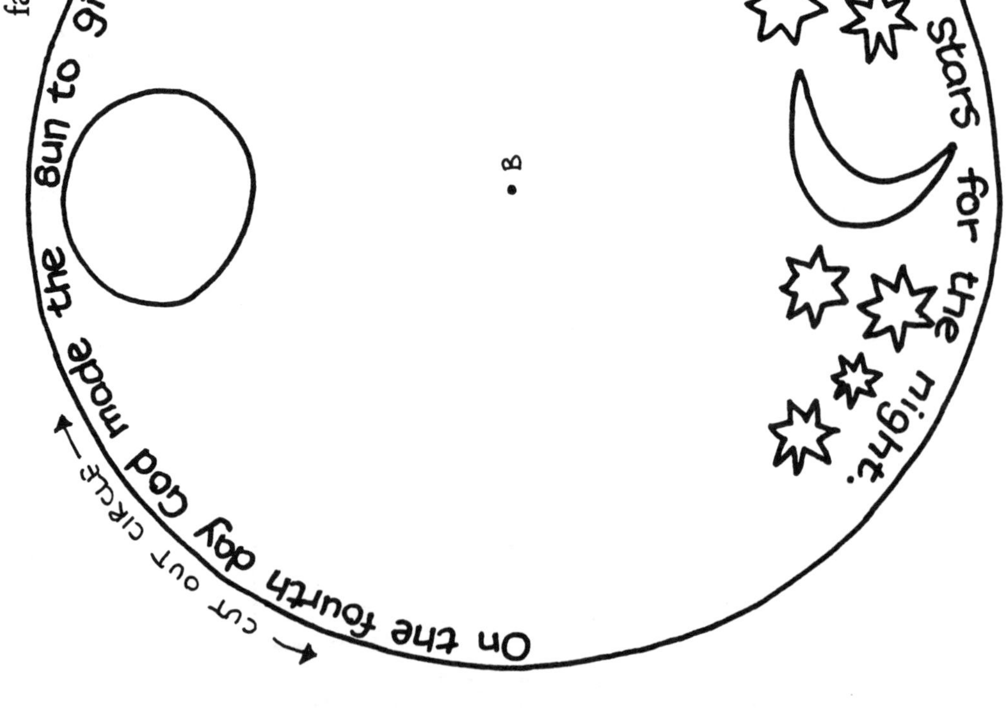

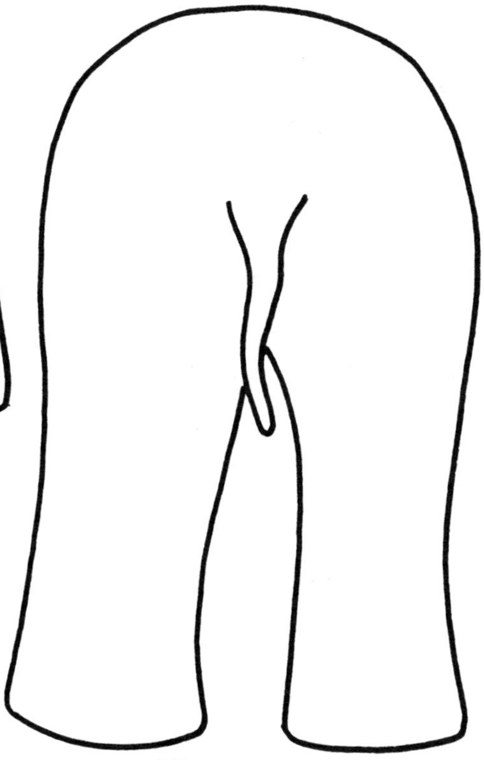

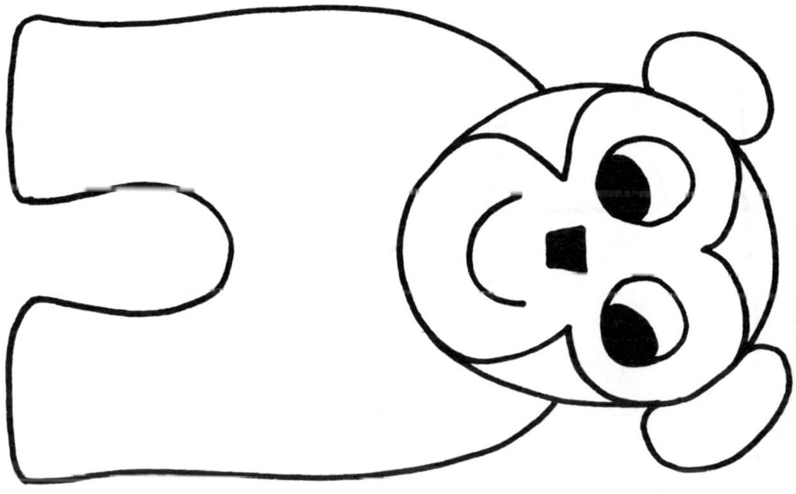

1. Photocopy onto thin card.
2. Colour in and cut out pieces.
3. Using two sticky fixers or glue, stick a cork between back and front of body – make sure feet are level. (Corks available from winemaking suppliers.)

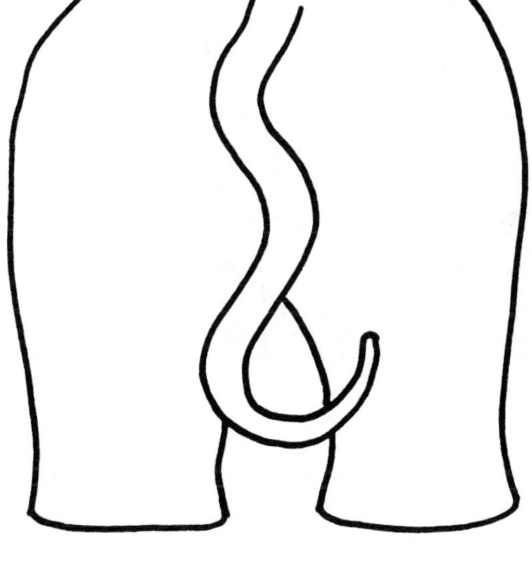

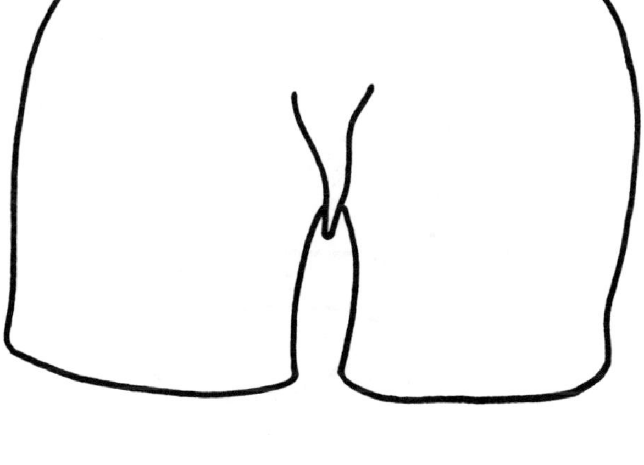

1. Photocopy onto thin card.
2. Colour and cut out.
3. Glue 'foot' circles together back to back.
4. Pierce dots A, B, C and D – put paper fastener through A, B, C and D.
5. Staple Abraham's head together.

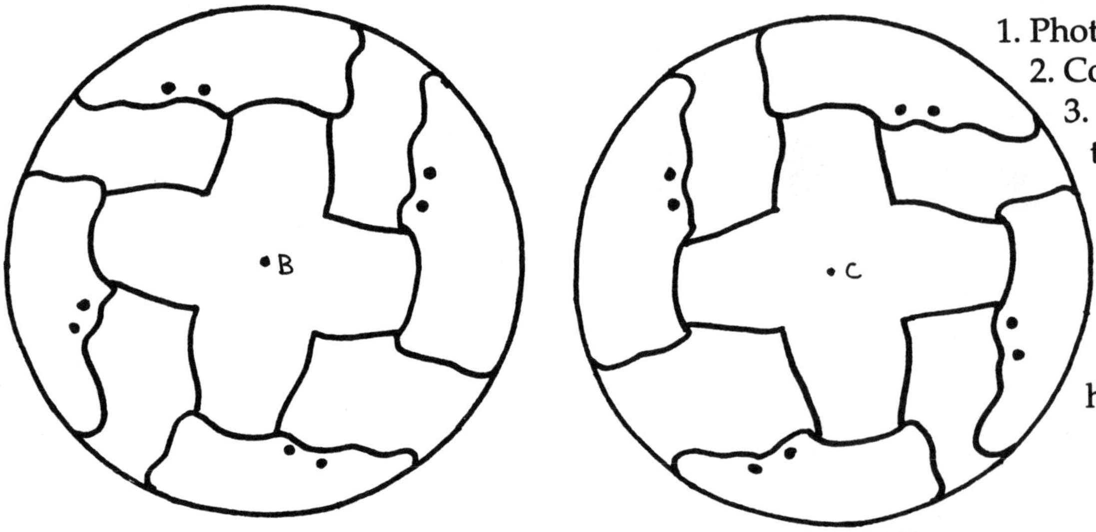

1. Photocopy onto thin card. 2. Colour in and cut out. 3. Glue well round into circle. 4. Fold tabs on well sides and glue on roof. 5. Slot pipecleaner through holes in well sides, bend for handle. Attach water pot on thread and wind up.

6. Stick Rebekah and servant to well.

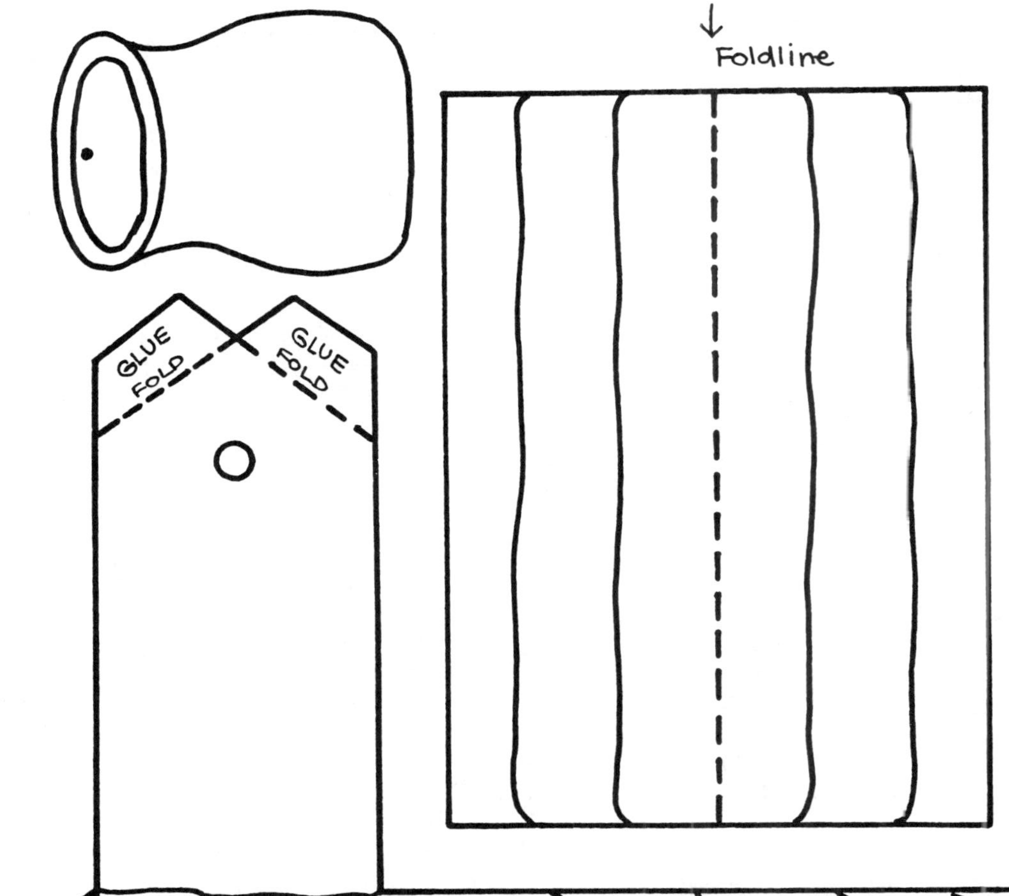

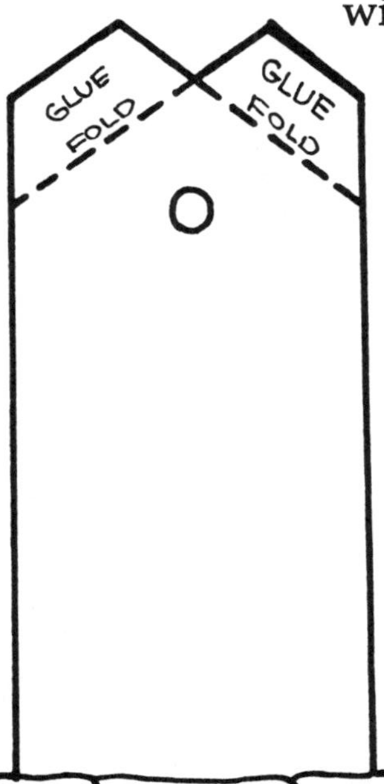

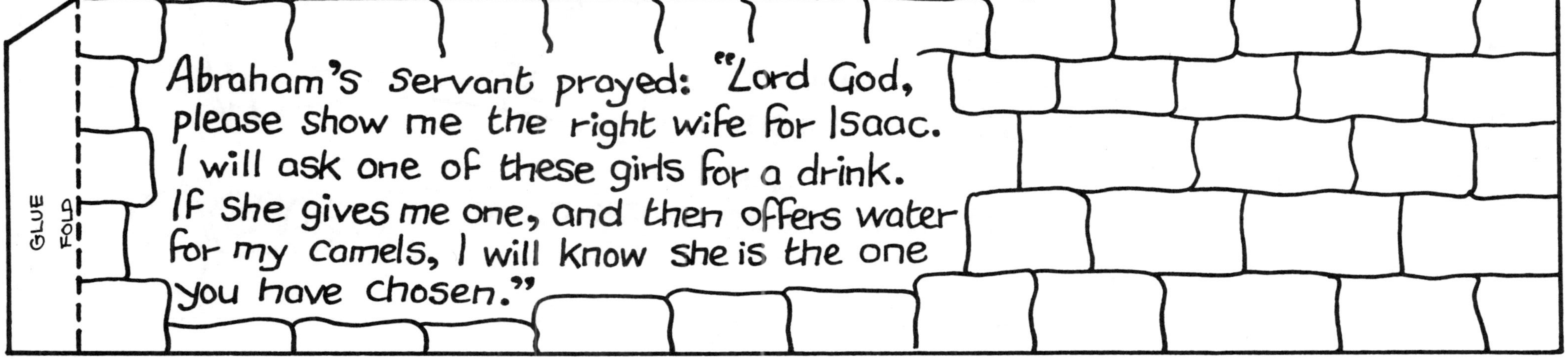

1. Photocopy onto thin card.
2. Colour and cut out.
3. Pierce dots A and B and attach arm with paper fastener through A and B
4. Attach 'Esau' clothes to Jacob with Blu-tack.

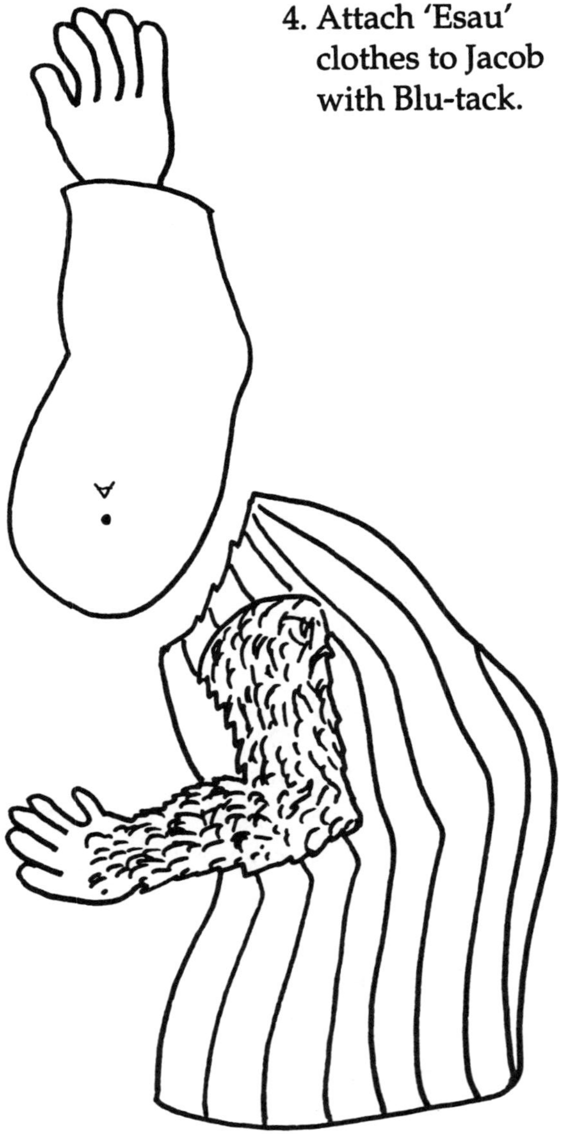

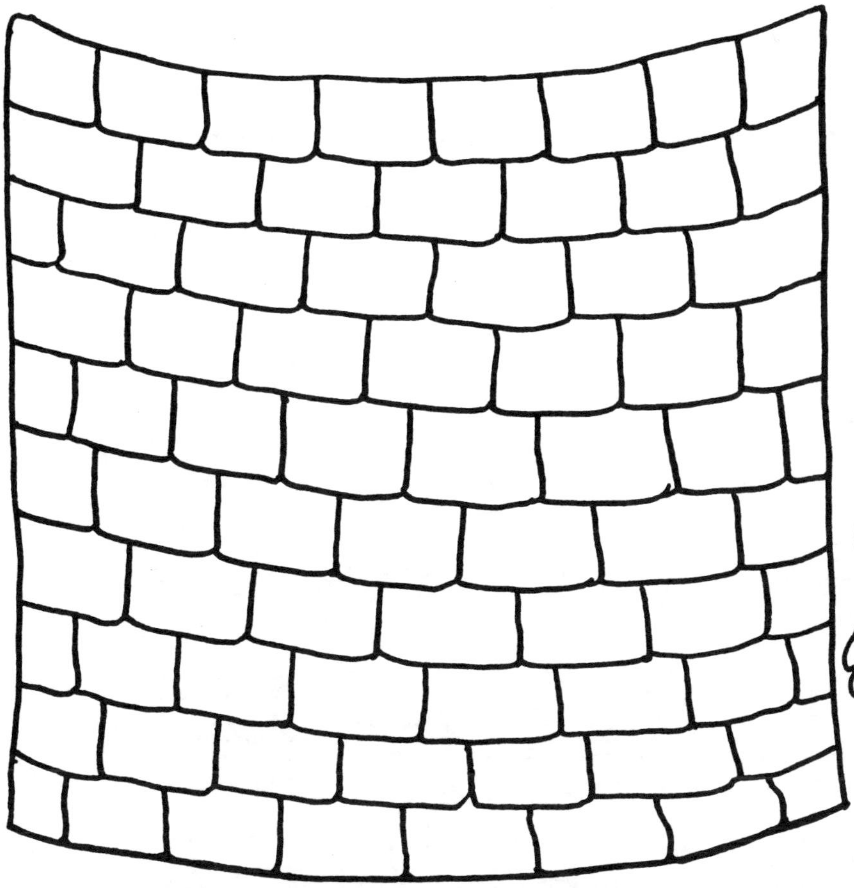

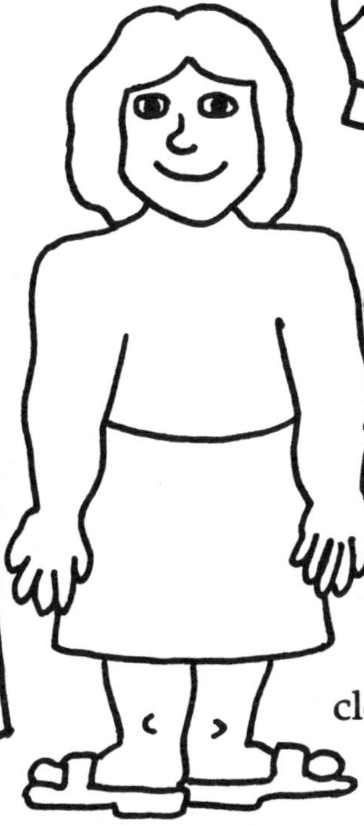

1. Photocopy onto thin card.
2. Colour and cut out.
3. Stick well onto picture – glue **edge** only.
4. Attach Joseph's clothes with Blu-tack – remove them to slot him into well.

1. Photocopy onto thin card. 2. Colour and cut out.
3. Fold on dotted lines to hide baby in basket.

1. Photocopy onto paper.
2. Draw a pattern on the snake.
3. Cut along black line to make spiral snake.
4. Hang up by thread attached to head.

1. Photocopy this and the following page onto thin card.
2. Colour and cut out.
3. Cut out three windows in top circle.
4. Pierce holes A and B then join the two circles with paper fastener through A then B.
5. Turn top circle to read off ten plagues.

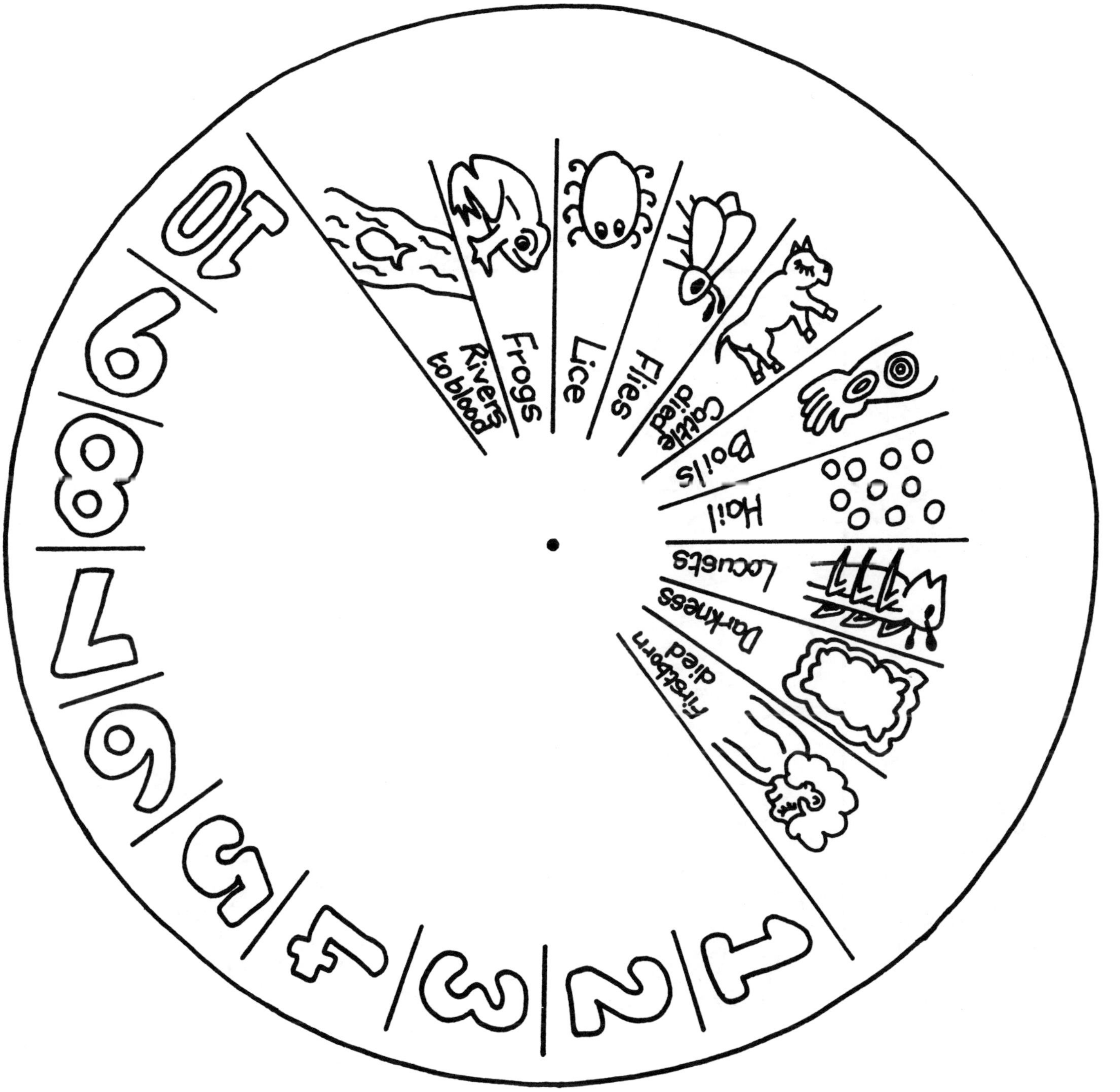

Rivers to blood
Frogs
Lice
Flies
Cattle died
Boils
Hail
Locusts
Darkness
Firstborn died
1
2
3
4
5
6
7
8
9
10

1. Photocopy onto thin card. 2. Colour and cut out – cut off strip with Moses and Egyptians. 3. Cut slits AB and CD and slot Moses and Egyptians strip through.
4. Glue waves XY and VW in place, so they open for Moses to go through.

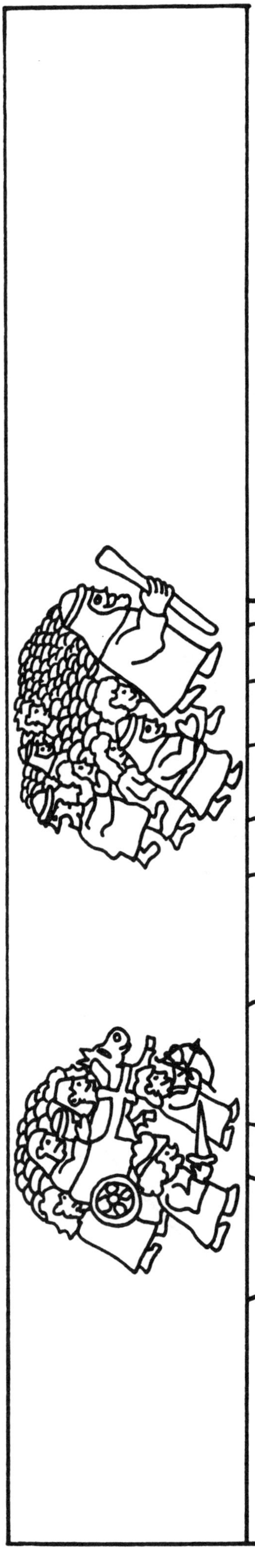

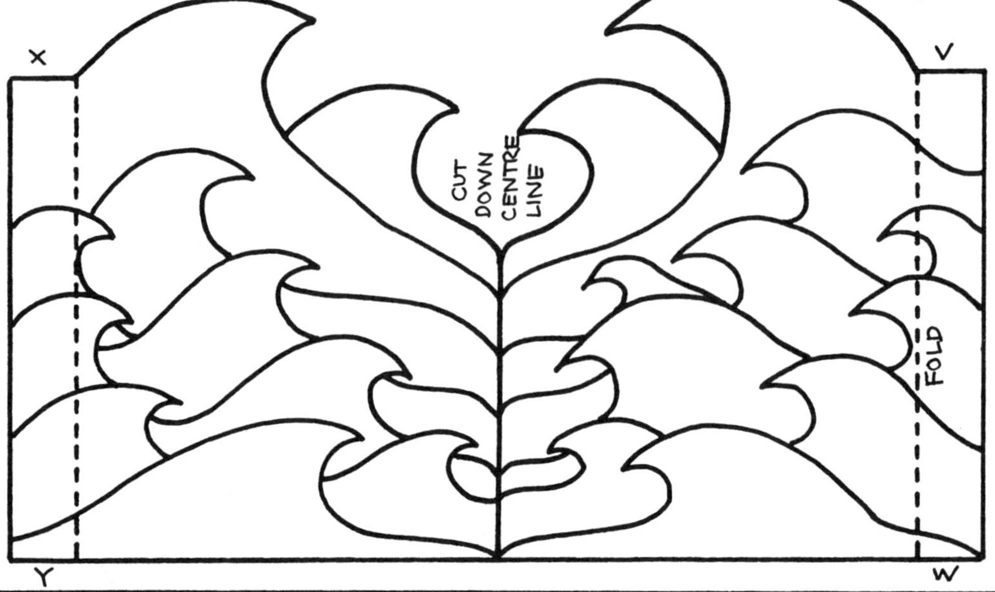

1. Photocopy onto thin card.
2. Colour and cut out.
3. Fold back all tabs on foldlines _ _ _ .
4. Glue city wall into circle and glue to base circle on dotted line . . .

5. Glue Joshua (standing upright) to short strip of card.
6. Pierce dots A and B and join B under A using a paper fastener.
7. Move strip of card round to make Joshua march round Jerico.

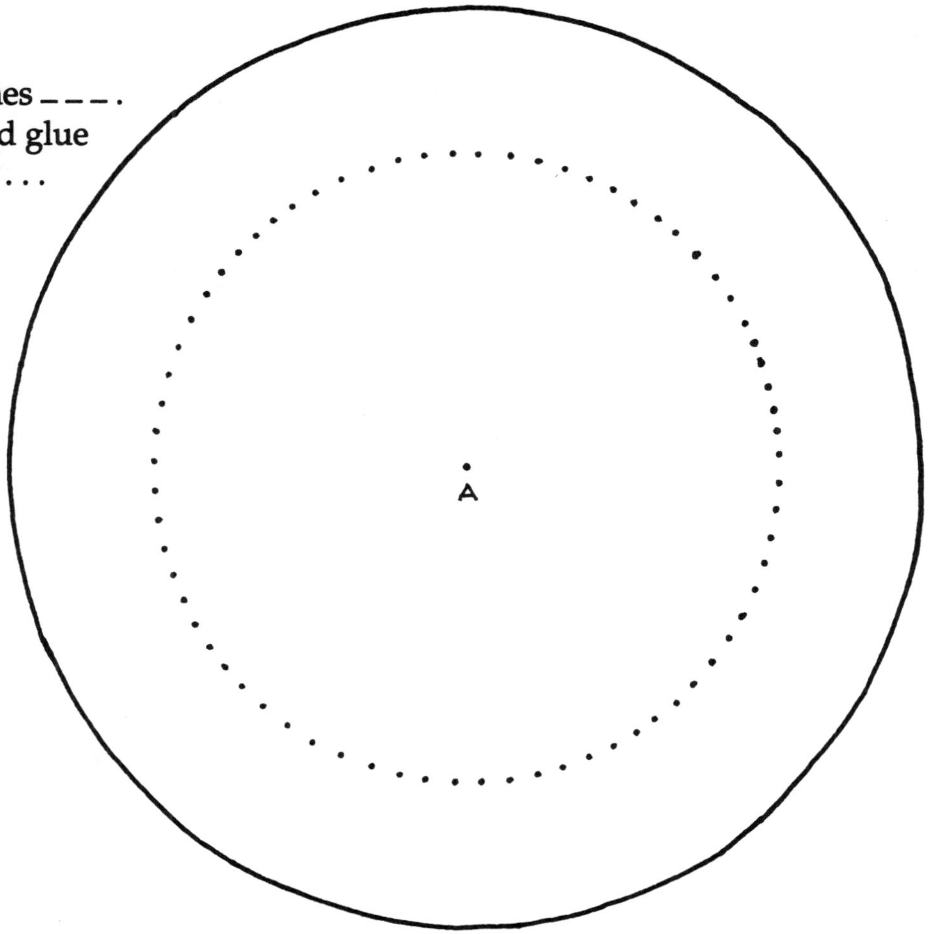

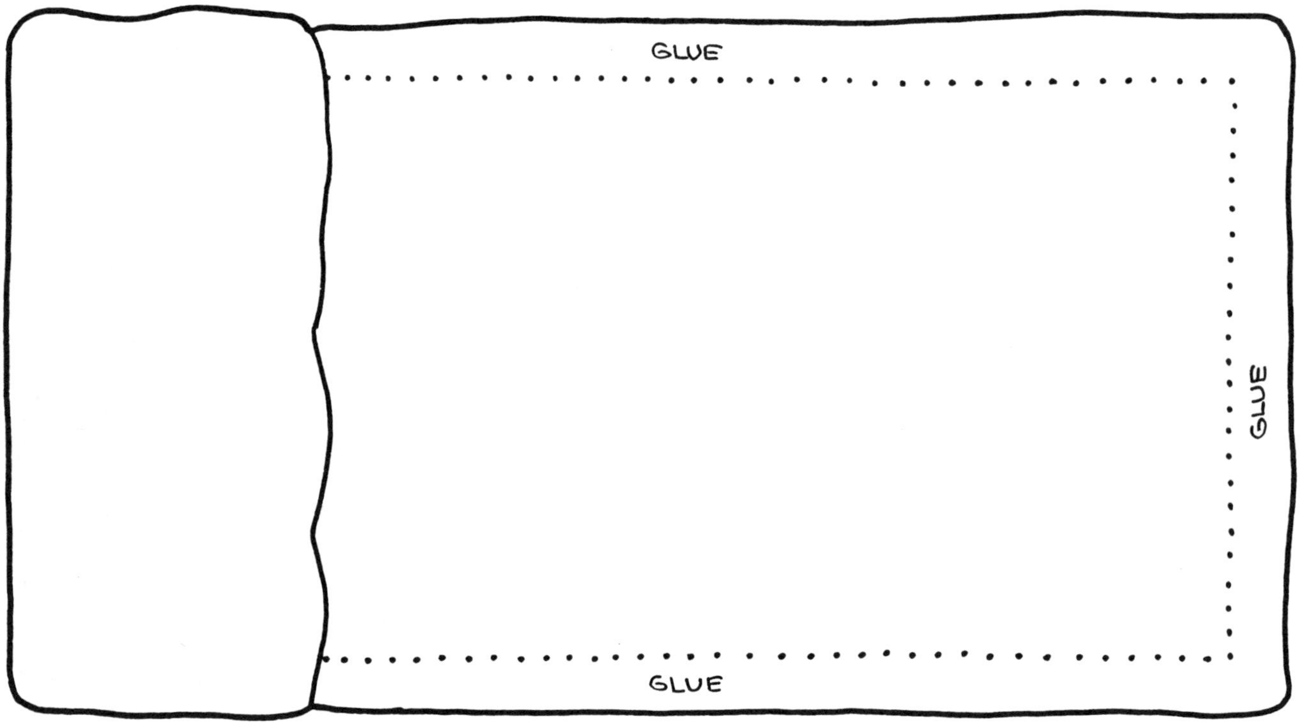

1. Photocopy onto thin card.
2. Colour and cut out.
3. Glue Samuel's sleeping bag together at **edges** only, as marked inside dotted line.
4. Slot Samuel into sleeping bag.

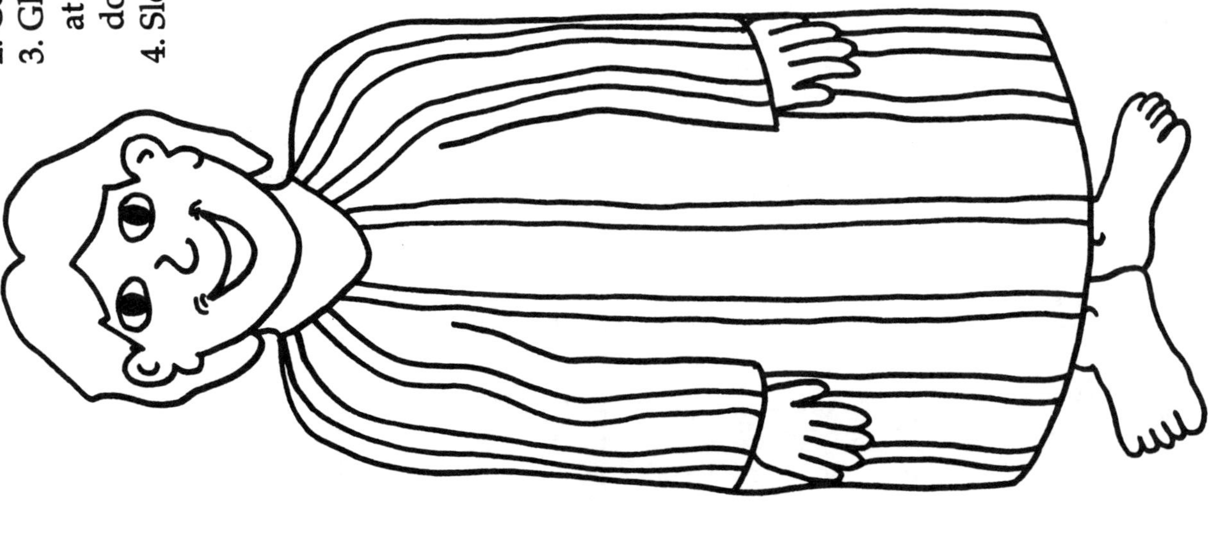

1. Photocopy onto thin card.
2. Colour and cut out.
3. Cut long slit on thick line on horn (AB).
4. Slot oil AB into slit AB
5. Move oil in and out as if pouring.

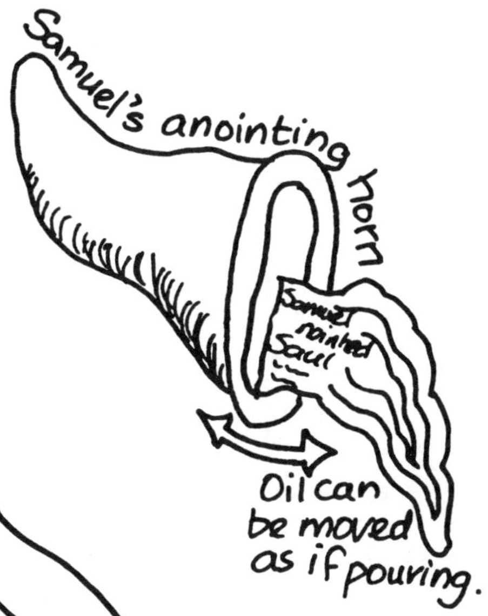

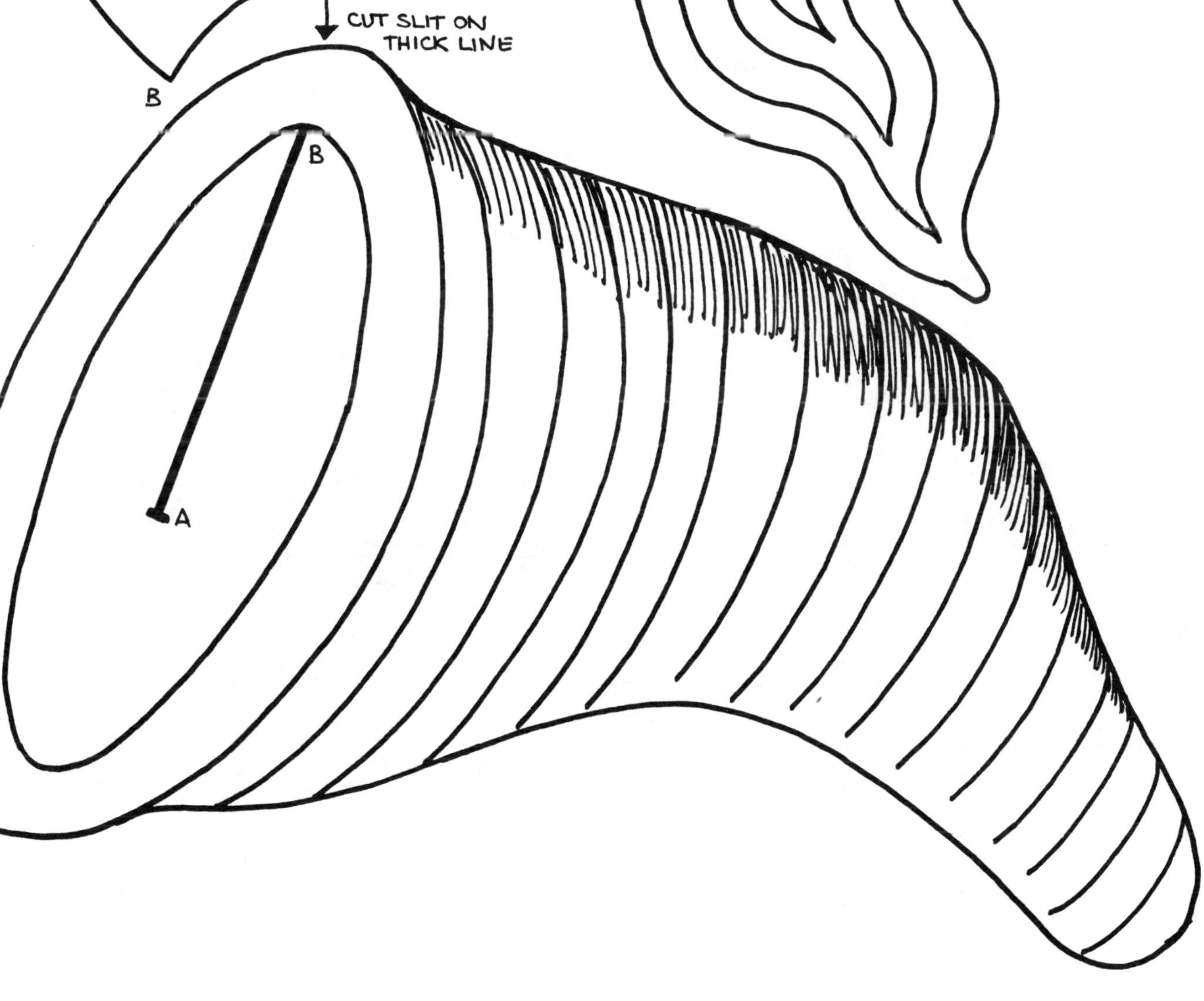

1. Photocopy onto thin card.
2. Colour and cut out.
3. On main picture cut two short slits WX and YZ.
4. Slot long slit with stone through WX from back, then YZ.
5. Pierce dots A and B; attach A over B with paper fastener.
6. Stone comes from sling, then Goliath topples.

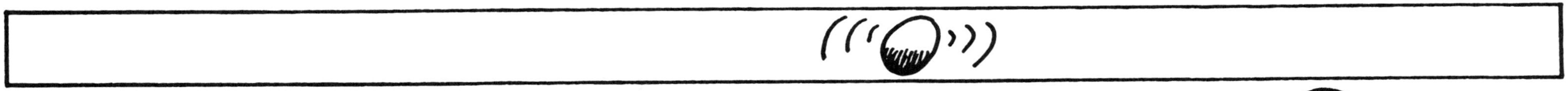

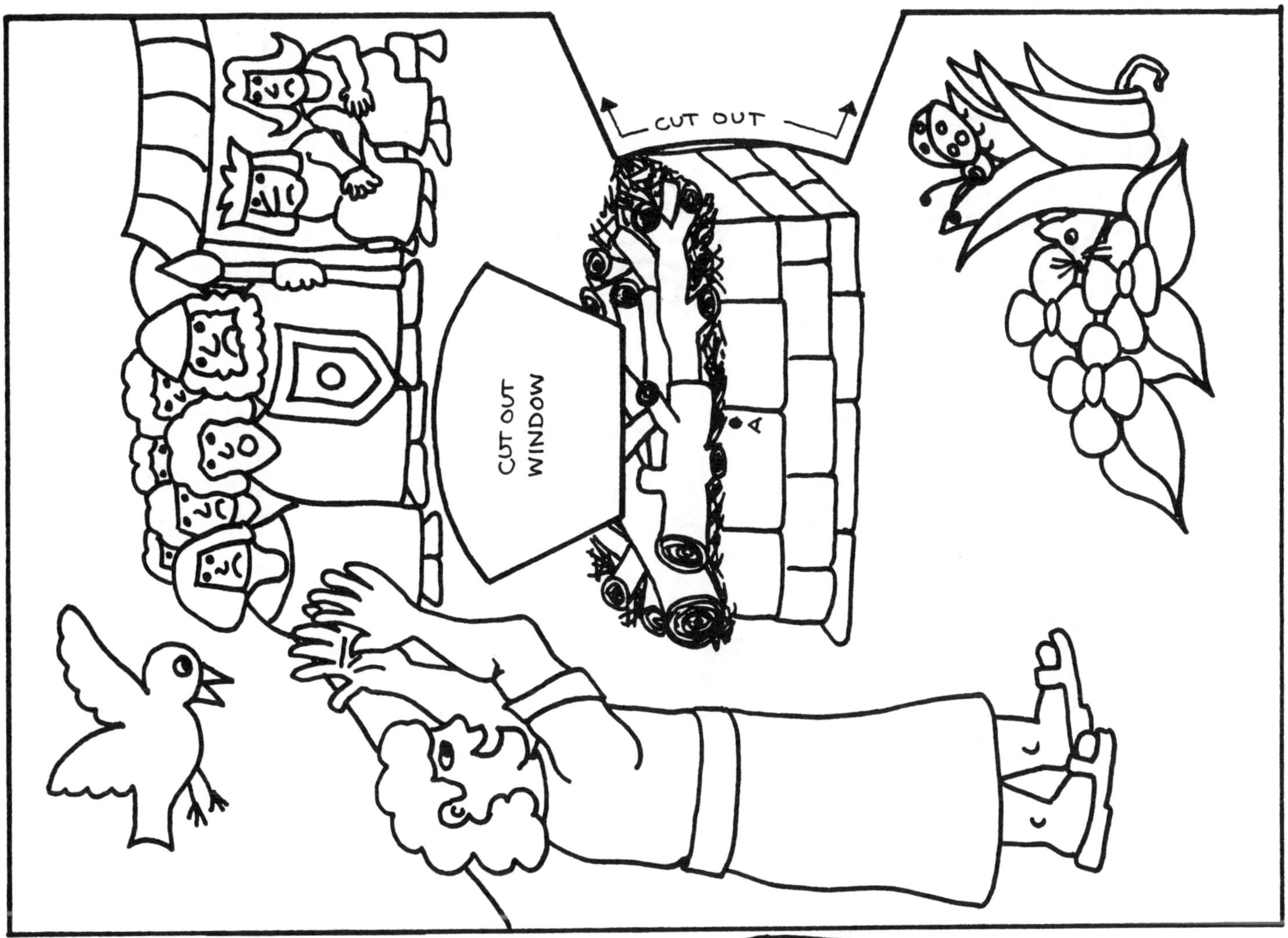

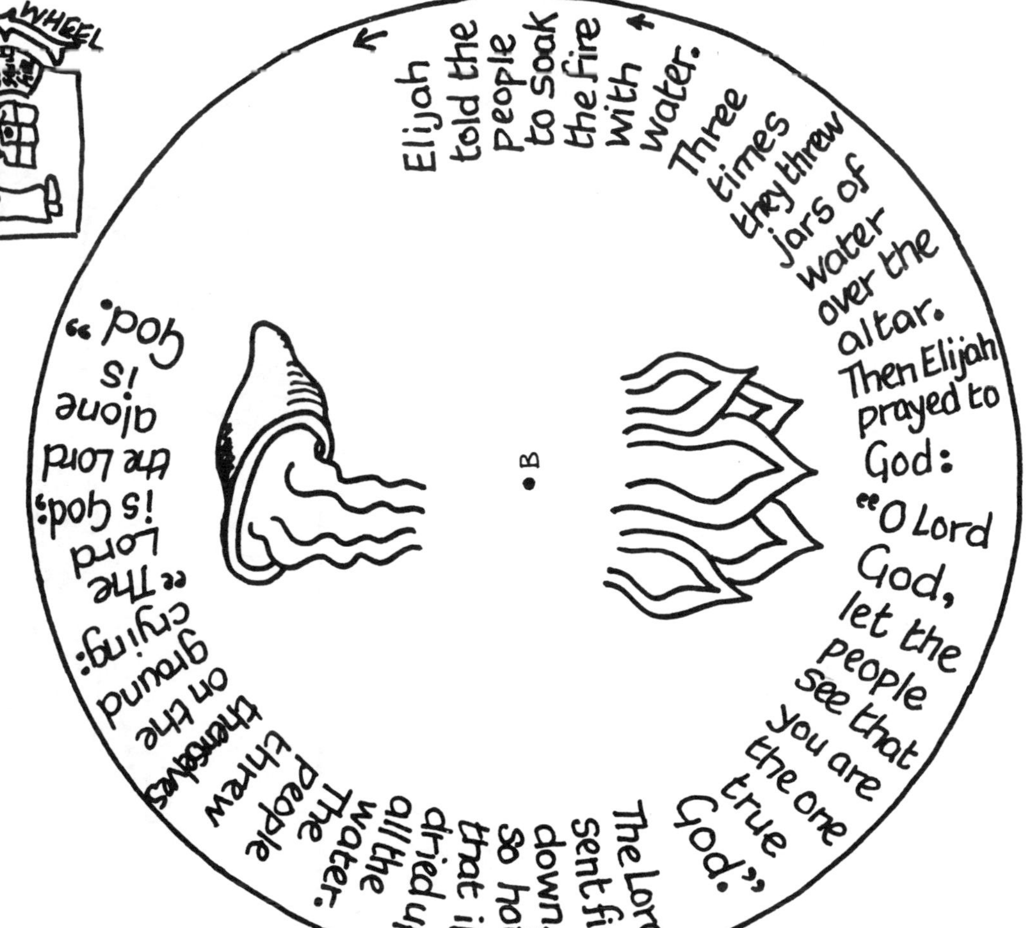

1. Photocopy onto thin card.
2. Colour and cut out.
3. Cut out window in main picture and notch at side.
4. Pierce holes A and B; attach B behind A using a paper fastener.
5. Turn wheel anticlockwise to read story.

1. Photocopy onto thin card.
2. Colour in and cut out – cut round outline of water.
3. Fold outwards on dotted lines.
4. Pierce dots A and B and attach B behind A using a paper fastener.
5. Glue large tab as marked and join to back piece of card.
6. Move Naaman in and out of water seven times to be healed.

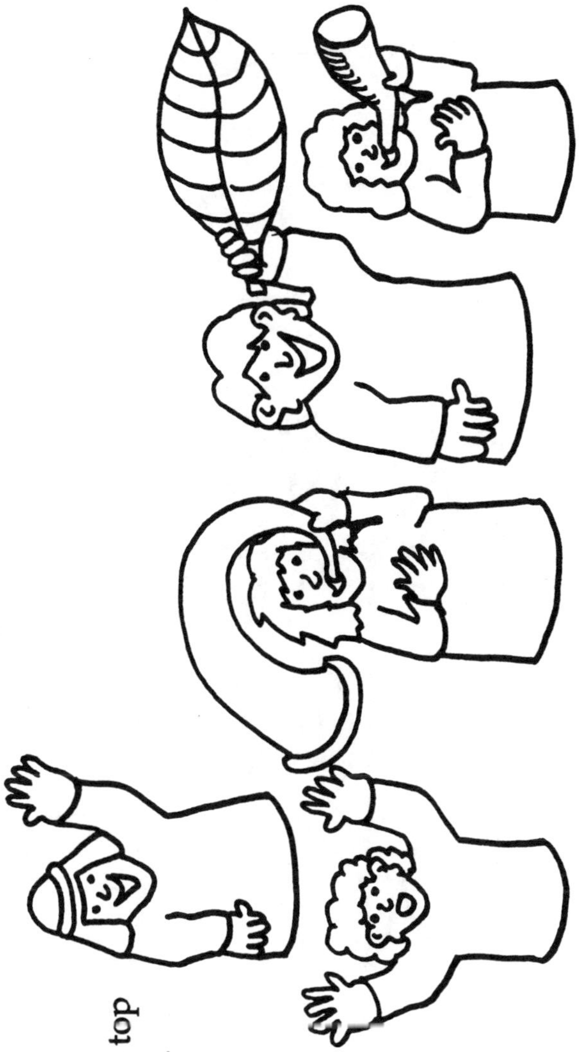

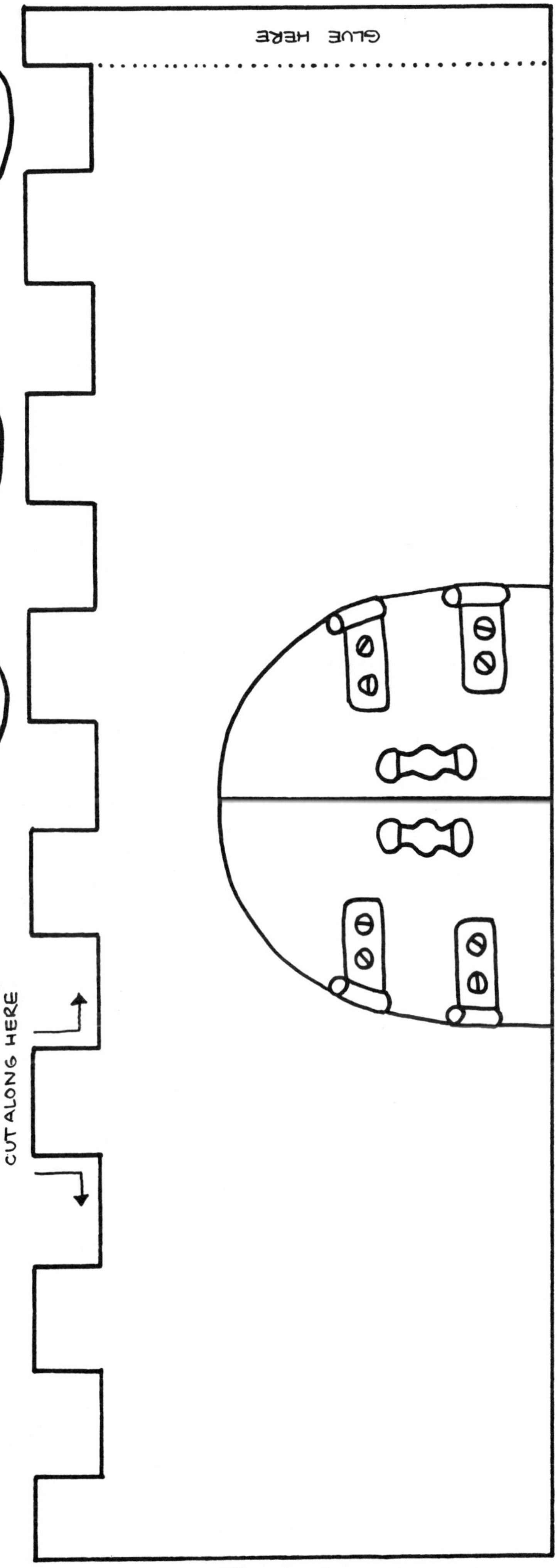

1. Photocopy onto thin card.
2. Colour and cut out city wall and people.
3. Write along top of city wall the words 'Everyone knew that the work had been done with God's help'.
4. Glue edge of city wall and stick together in circle.
5. Stick the people praising God around the top **inside** edge of city wall, facing outwards.

Shadrach, Meshach and Abednego said:

"The God we serve is able to save us from the fiery furnace."

CUT RIGHT ALONG THIS LINE

1. Photocopy onto thin card.
2. Colour in and cut along solid black outer lines.
3. Cut six vertical slits on furnace marked I.
4. Slot strip with picture of three friends, in and out of the six slits, as shown in small diagram.

5. Pull strip through from left to right to see the three friends walk through the fiery furnace.

1. Photocopy onto thin card.
2. Colour and cut out main picture and all plates of food and hand.
3. Cut down solid vertical lines AB and CD.
4. Fold outwards on dotted line marked – – – and inwards on dotted lines marked –.–.–.–. so that the table stands out from wall (scoring lines first helps).
5. Stick food on table and hand on wall.
6. Write words on wall – Mene, mene, tekel, parsin.

1. Photocopy onto thin card. 2. Colour and cut out lion mask.
3. Cut out eye holes.
4. Pierce at A and B and re-inforce with self-adhesive plastic washers.
5. Tie a length of shirring elastic through these holes to go round back of head.

SUGGESTION
You could act out the story – but remember that the lions were not fierce to Daniel!

1. Photocopy onto thin card.
2 Colour and cut out whale and Jonah – cut hole in middle of whale.
3. Pierce dots A and B and hang Jonah inside whale using shirring elastic or thread.
4. Find balance point at top of whale and pierce hole – hang up mobile using shirring elastic.

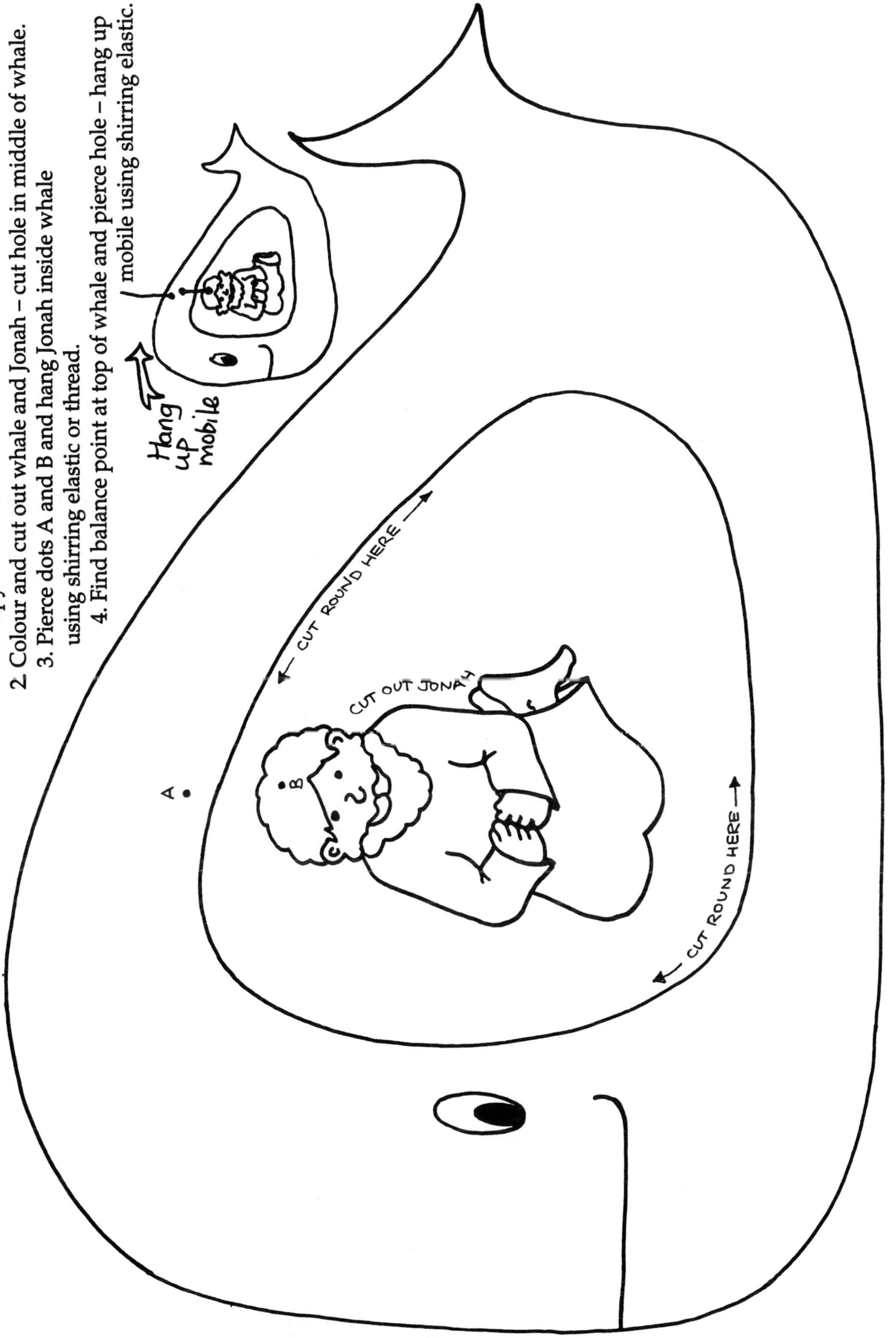

JOHN THE BAPTIST

LISTENING

(cf Matthew 3:1-11)

John the Baptist went to live in the desert. He wore a coat made from camel hair, tied around the middle with a belt. The desert was too hot and dry for many things to grow, so John lived on wild honey and locusts. God had told him that he was sending someone special to save the world. He wanted John to tell everyone that they must change their ways and try to become good. People came from far and wide to be baptised by John in the River Jordan. They wanted to say sorry for all their sins. One day John told them, 'I can wash you with water, but a very special person is coming who will baptise you with God's Spirit and wash away all your sins.'

TALKING

Where did John the Baptist go to live?

In the desert. (Discuss what a desert is like. Show pictures if possible.)

What did he wear? Do you think his coat was very comfortable?

Can anyone remember what John had to eat in the desert?

(Make sure the children know what a locust is!)

What was the message that God wanted John to tell the people?

God wanted John to tell all the people to change their ways and become good, because he was sending Jesus to be their king.

DOING

Photocopy the picture of John in the desert and ask the children to colour this in.

OR

In advance prepare a large picture of John the Baptist. Make copies of the locusts and the honey pot. Using glue-sticks, glue John's coat, and encourage the children to sprinkle on sawdust, sand, porridge oats or any other material to represent the rough camel hair. Alternatively glue patches of coarse material or fabric into place. The remainder of the group can colour the honey pots and locusts which complete the picture.

PRAYING

Heavenly Father, you sent John the Baptist
to prepare the people for the coming of Jesus.
Help us to prepare, too,
to welcome Jesus into our hearts.

Wild
honey

FOLLOW ME!

LISTENING

(cf Matthew 4:12-23)

After Jesus had been baptised by John, he went to live in Capernaum, a fishing village beside the Sea of Galilee. One day he saw two brothers, called Simon Peter and Andrew, out fishing together. Jesus spoke to them and they were filled with wonder when he said, 'Come and follow me and I will make you fishers of men and women.' The two brothers left their boat and nets at once, and followed him. A little further on Jesus saw James and John, out fishing with their father, Zebedee. Again, Jesus asked them to follow him, and they left their father and went with him. These brothers were the first disciples of Jesus.

TALKING

What were the names of the brothers in the story?

What did they do for a living?

What do you think Zebedee thought when his sons went off with Jesus?

Jesus was obviously a very special person. Something about him was so different, they were prepared to leave everything and to follow him.

What did Jesus mean when he said that he would make them 'fishers of men and women'?

They would help to spread the message of God's love which Jesus had brought. They would gather the people to Jesus as fishermen gather all the fish into one net! These people would learn to know and love Jesus too, and would follow him.

Does Jesus want us to follow him too?

Sometimes people today give up everything to follow Jesus.

How can we follow him every day?

By the way we live and treat others:

- being kind and good
- following his rules
- loving God and all his people

We can show how much we love Jesus by the way we behave, and that may make other people want to know about Jesus too.

DOING

Cut out a fish shape for each child to colour and write their name on. Place each fish in a net (using a vegetable or fruit bag) and then pin this onto a background scene on the board to complete the picture.

Alternatively the children can complete the photocopied picture adding as many varied and colourful fish as they like and finally drawing a net over them all which is attached to the rope.

PRAYING

Jesus, help us to listen
when you ask us to follow you.
May we walk beside you each day
and share your love with those we meet
so that they will want to follow you too.

1. Photocopy onto thin card (this page).
2. Colour in lettering and cut out.
3. See page two of model for further instructions.

1. Photocopy this page onto **paper** – if possible, a contrasting colour to the card on page 1.
2. Join dots of lettering – in rainbow colours if you like!
3. Cut out.
4. Fold 'the precious pearl' card outwards and stick paper circle with lettering inside.

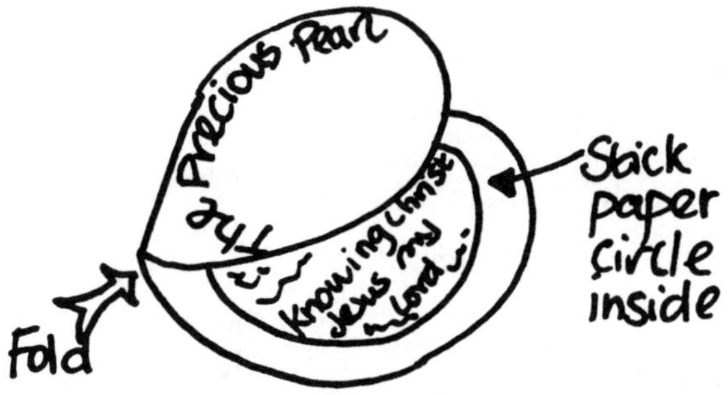

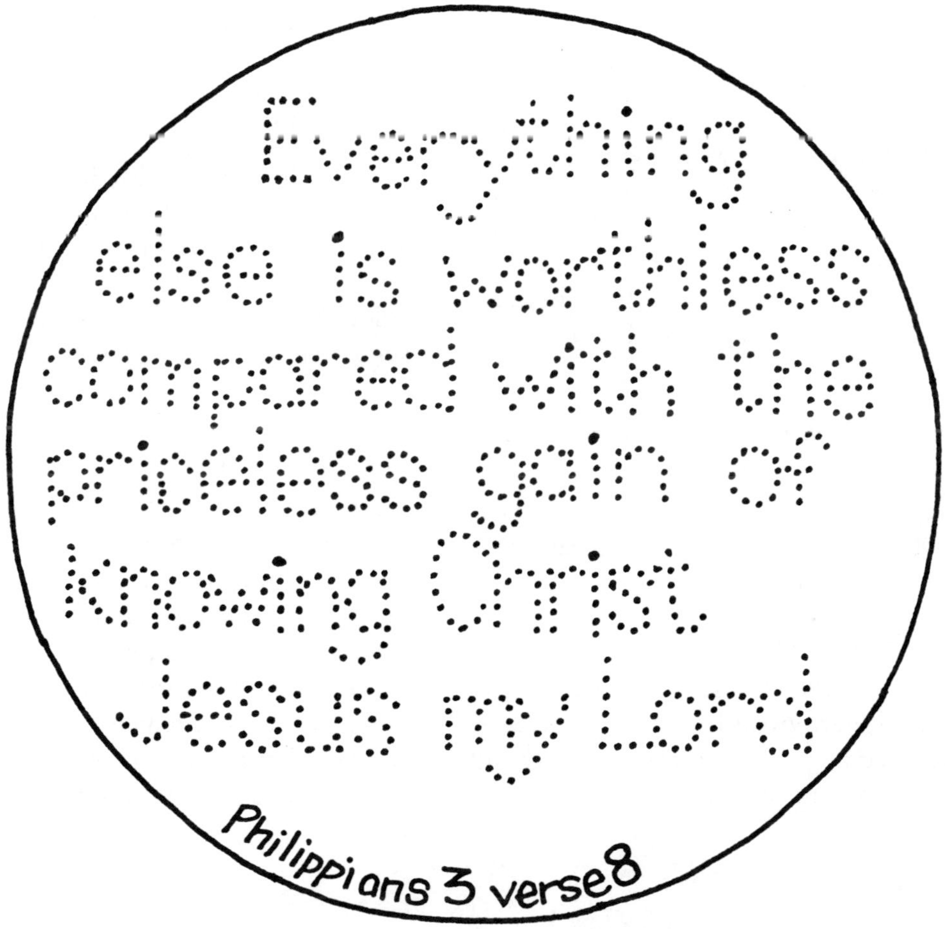

MATTHEW THE TAX COLLECTOR

READING

(cf Matthew 9:9-13)

One day as Jesus was walking along he saw a man called Matthew who was a tax collector. He went over to him and said, 'Follow me.' Matthew did as Jesus told him. They went to Matthew's house where Jesus stayed for supper. Many other tax collectors came and shared the meal with Jesus and his disciples. Jesus overheard a Pharisee asking one of his disciples, 'Why is your master friendly with such dishonest and unkind people?'

Jesus turned to him and said, 'Good people do not need my help. It is people such as these tax collectors who need me; I will forgive them and call them to follow me.'

DISCUSSION

Tax collectors were hated by the Jews, do you know why?

The people had to give a part of any money they earned to the Roman government in taxes. People like Matthew collected the taxes from the people, and often charged them extra money which they kept for themselves. The Jews hated them because they worked for the Romans and were often dishonest.

When Jesus asked Matthew to become a follower, do you think everyone was surprised?

Matthew was greedy and selfish, ready to cheat and take their money. Everyone was amazed that Jesus wanted to befriend this man.

What did the Pharisees say?

Pharisees were Jews who strictly obeyed the Jewish law and were proud of their goodness. They disapproved because Jesus chose to befriend a sinner rather than one of them.

Matthew was not a good man, but are any of us good all the time?

Just because we are not good all the time, Jesus does not stop being our friend. He wanted us to see people like Matthew with God's loving eyes. Not to judge them and to turn away, but to reach out and forgive them.

Do you think that meeting Jesus changed Matthew's life?

Jesus changed the lives of everyone he met. His love and goodness spread to those around him, and they in turn shared it with others. When Matthew followed Jesus that day, his life changed direction as he walked in the footsteps of Jesus, and he realised how selfish and dishonest he had been. Jesus was willing to offer forgiveness and friendship so that Matthew could make a fresh start in life! Matthew had a change of heart.

ACTIVITY

Cut out the figure of Matthew and a set of clothes with which to 'dress' him. These can be coloured and decorated as befits a wealthy man. Stick several bags of gold to a belt on his waist. After colouring, stick the heart shape onto his chest, to show that Matthew had a change of heart.

CLOSING PRAYER

Dear Jesus,
you were ready to forgive Matthew
and offer him your friendship,
just as your heavenly Father
is always ready to forgive us
and let us make a fresh start.
Help us always to remember this,
so that we are ready to forgive
those we meet on our journey through life.

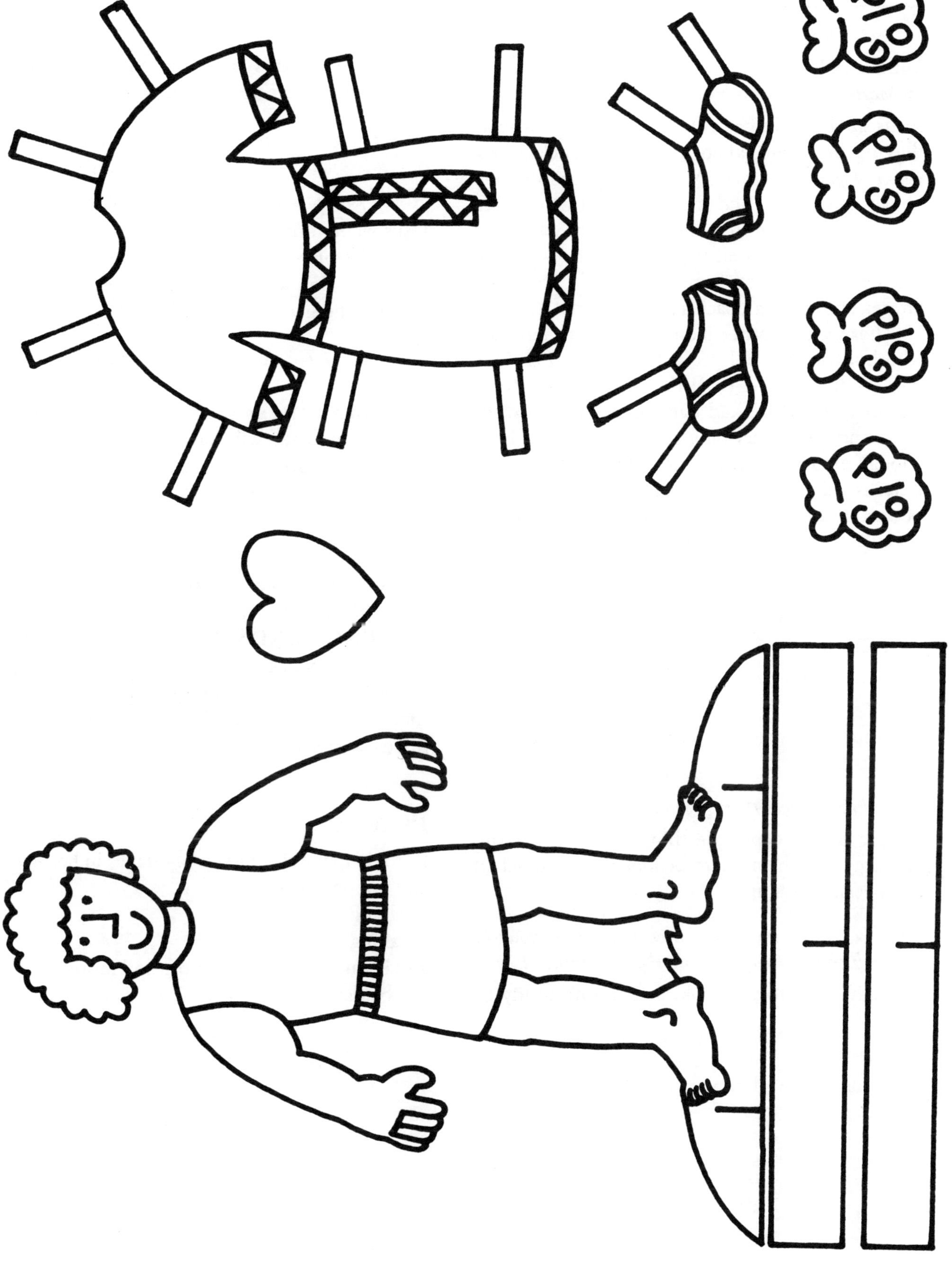

Priceless treasure

Listening

(cf Matthew 13:44-46)

Jesus said to the crowds, 'One day a man was digging in a field when his spade struck a box which was buried there. When he opened the box he was amazed to find it was full of treasure. He quickly buried the treasure again, went away and sold his house and all that he owned. With the money he made, he bought the field from the farmer, and then ran back and dug up the treasure.

'There was another man who was a merchant who bought and sold pearls to earn a living. One day he happened to find the most perfect, beautiful pearl he had ever seen. He too went away and sold everything so that he would have enough money to buy that pearl for himself.'

Jesus said, 'God's kingdom is the real treasure, as perfect and precious as the pearl; you would give up everything you have for it, because it is worth more than anything else in the whole world.'

Talking

Do your parents have things which are very precious to them?

A favourite ornament, a piece of jewellery, a car or a picture.

How do they treat these precious things?

People often keep these things safe from harm, and only take them out to be looked at or touched on special occasions.

Do you have something which is very precious to you, which you treasure more than anything else?

It might be a toy, a book, a favourite teddy or some item which is not important to other people but means a great deal to you.

Like the grown ups, do you treat your 'treasure' carefully because it means so much to you?

Would you be willing to give it away or swap it?

Jesus wanted us to understand that God's love for us is like priceless treasure. It means more than any possession we have on earth; it is worth giving up everything we own in order to have it.

What must we do to find the treasure of God's kingdom?

By living as Jesus taught us and loving and trusting him, we will have God's love, which is worth more than anything else in the world.

Doing

Cut out the large 'treasure chest' and several 'jewels'. Label the jewels with words like SHARING, KINDNESS, FRIENDLINESS and add your own ideas. (Let the children suggest others.) Decorate the jewels imaginatively! Label the chest 'God's kingdom' and fill it with the priceless jewels.

Praying

Lord, help me to store up my riches in heaven
and not on earth,
by doing what is good,
speaking what is true
and learning to love you more and more
day by day.

GOD'S
KINGDOM

HAVE FAITH

READING

(cf Matthew 14:22-33)

Before going up to the hills to pray alone, Jesus told his disciples to sail to the other side of the lake. As night fell, the wind grew stronger and the disciples' boat was tossed about by the waves. Suddenly they saw someone coming towards the boat, walking on the water, and they were terrified, because they thought it was a ghost! But Jesus called to them, 'Don't be afraid, it's me!'

Peter shouted to Jesus, 'Lord, if that really is you, tell me to come to you across the water.'

'Come!' said Jesus.

So Peter climbed out of the boat and lowered himself onto the water. Looking straight at Jesus, he began to walk towards him, but as he moved further from the boat and felt the strength of the wind, he grew afraid. Suddenly he began to sink and he cried out, 'Save me, Jesus!' As Jesus reached out his hand and pulled Peter to safety he said, 'Why did you not trust me Peter? Is your belief so weak?' When they got back to the boat, the other disciples knelt before Jesus and said, 'You are truly the Son of God.'

DISCUSSION

At first, what did the disciples think they had seen coming across the water towards them?

A ghost.

What did they do?

Imagine how frightened they must have been to suddenly see someone walking on top of the water towards them on a dark stormy night. They probably cried out in fear and tried to hide somewhere on the boat.

What did Jesus do to calm their fears?

He said, 'Do not be afraid.' Jesus said this on several other occasions when the disciples were frightened by some of the amazing things they saw. Remember when he appeared to them in the upper room after his death, and again said, 'Do not be afraid.'

What did Peter do when he heard Jesus calling him to come?

Peter climbed out of the boat and began to walk towards Jesus!

Can an ordinary person normally walk on water?

We can swim in water and we can lie and float in the water, but if we try to stand without anything to make us float we only sink.

What was so special about Peter that allowed him to walk on the water towards Jesus?

Peter was full of courage and faith. He was the first one to realise that Jesus was truly the Son of God.

What happened to Peter when he felt the strength of the wind?

He began to sink beneath the waves, because for just a moment his faith and belief weakened and he felt afraid. Sometimes we are like Peter, full of courage and enthusiasm at first, but often let down by our lack of faith and by fear of the unknown.

What did Jesus do?

Peter was an ordinary person like us, and he would often let Jesus down because his faith was weak. (Remember how he denied Jesus three times after his arrest.) Jesus is always forgiving and ready to reach out his hand to save us just as he reached out that night and saved Peter on the lake.

ACTIVITY

Use squares of coloured paper to make boats with masts and sails.

CLOSING PRAYER

Lord, give us the courage and faith of Peter,
whose belief was so strong
that he could walk towards Jesus across the lake.
In times of weakness,
reach out your hand to us
and rescue us from our doubts.

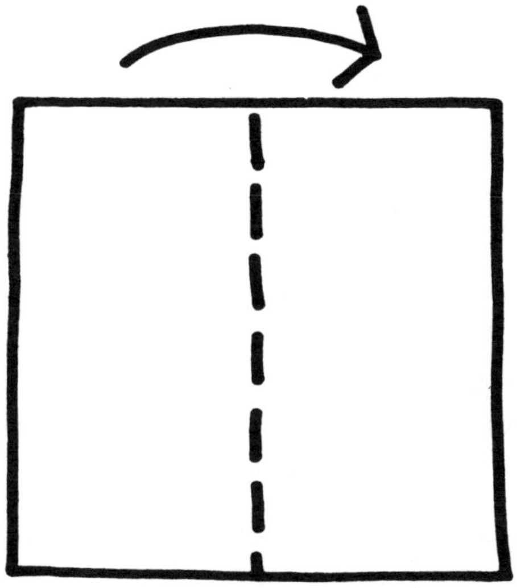

1.Fold square of paper in half.

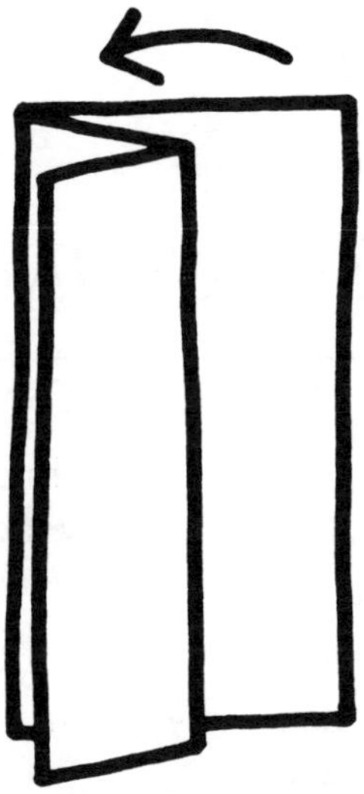

2.Fold edge of paper back to meet folded edge.

3.Turn paper over and repeat action. Then unfold paper.

4.Fold corners into middle crease.

5.Fold right edge over to folded edge.

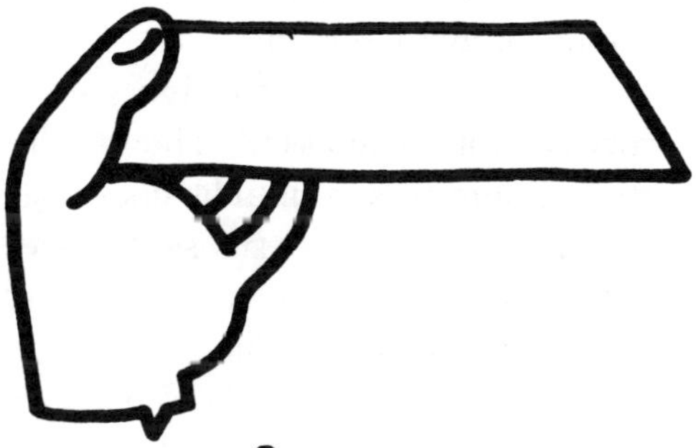

6.Put fingers inside and push corners down with thumbs to make boat 'stand'.

7.

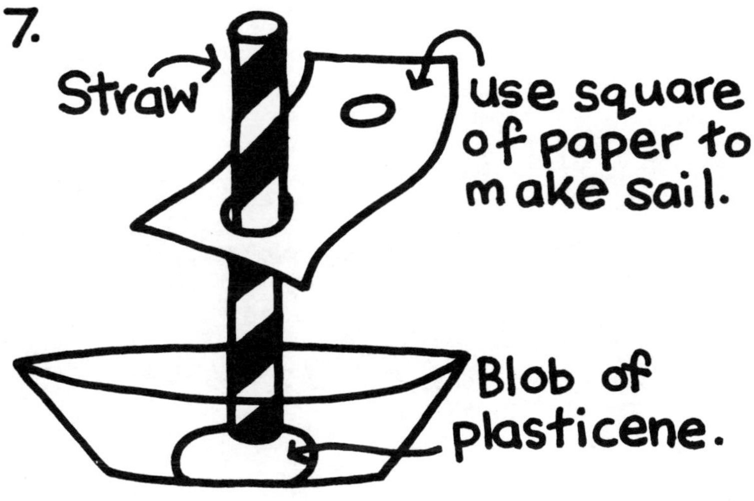

8.

Be forgiving

Reading

(cf Matthew 18:23-35)

One day Jesus said, 'There was once a king who had many servants. One servant owed the king a great deal of money, but he had nothing to pay him with. "I will sell you and your family as slaves, and use the money to pay for your debts," said the king.

'The servant fell to his knees and begged for another chance. "Somehow I will repay everything I owe," he pleaded. The king was a kind and generous man and, taking pity on the servant, cancelled his debts and let him go.

'Later that day, the servant met another man who owed him a small amount of money. When he could not pay what he owed, the servant had him thrown into jail.

'When the news reached the king, he sent for the unforgiving servant.

'"Could you not forgive someone just as I forgave you?" he asked. Then he had the servant thrown into prison until he could pay back all that he owed the king.' Jesus said, 'Just as my Father forgives you, so you must be ready to forgive others with all your heart.'

Discussion

Why was the servant in trouble with the king?

At first what did the king do?

He said he would sell the servant and his family as slaves to pay off his debts.

What did he do instead?

Even though the servant owed him a great deal of money, he completely forgave his debt and gave him the chance to make a fresh start.

Did the servant show the same forgiveness towards the man who owed him some money?

He quickly forgot the good example shown by the king and what a difference the king's mercy had made to his life.

What happened to the unforgiving servant?

The angry king had him thrown into jail until he could repay all that he owed.

What message does Jesus give us in this parable?

That we must be ready to forgive others, however large or small their wrongdoing, if we want to be forgiven ourselves.

God will always forgive us but in the same way he expects us to show mercy to others.

Activity

Photocopy the series of pictures telling today's parable. After colouring, pin them on a board for the children to look at and discuss.

Closing Prayer

Jesus taught us a prayer that mentions how we must forgive others when we ask forgivenss ourselves. Listen closely to the words that speak of forgiveness:
Our Father . . .

THE
UNFORGIVING
SERVANT

PALM SUNDAY

LISTENING

(cf Matthew 21:1-11)

Jesus and his disciples arrived at the Mount of Olives just outside Jerusalem. He sent two of the disciples to the next village to collect a donkey and her foal. 'If anyone stops you, tell them that they are for me,' he said. They brought the animals to Jesus, and put cloaks on their backs so that Jesus could ride on them. When the people heard that Jesus was coming they laid their cloaks on the road before him, and pulled branches off the palm trees to wave in the air. The crowds grew more and more excited and shouted at the top of their voices, 'Hosanna, Hosanna! Blessed is the one sent by the Lord.' Excitement filled the whole city, and some people asked, 'Who is this man?' The people answered them, 'It is Jesus from Nazareth in Galilee.'

TALKING

What did Jesus ask his friends to fetch from the village?

Would you expect a king to ride on a little donkey or a grand horse?

Why did Jesus choose a donkey?

By his actions Jesus was showing the crowds that he was no soldier, but instead he came as a king of peace, riding on a meek and gentle donkey.

What did the crowds wave in their hands and what words did they use to cheer as he passed?

They waved branches from the palm trees they found along the roadside to welcome their king, just as we might wave flags in a procession today. They shouted 'Hosanna, Hosanna!' – which is a word used to praise God.

DOING

Enlarge the figure of Jesus on a donkey and photocopy onto thin card. The children can then make the decoration of the figure and donkey colourful and imaginative! Then fix another piece of card to make the figure free-standing. Other children can be involved in making newspaper 'palms' to lay before the finished model of Jesus on the donkey.

PRAYING

Lord Jesus, Prince of Peace and King of the world,
we pray that your peace
will spread throughout the world today
and touch the lives of everyone.

1.
NEWS
2.
3.
4.
5.
6

Be ready

Reading

(cf Matthew 25:1-13)

One day Jesus told this parable, 'Ten bridesmaids were getting ready for a wedding, and together they went to greet the bridegroom, although they were not sure when he would come, or how long they would have to wait. Five of them were sensible girls who brought flasks of oil to refill their lamps; the other girls did not. The bridegroom was late, and after waiting all afternoon and all evening, the bridesmaids finally fell asleep. It was already midnight when somebody cried, "The bridegroom is coming! Quickly go and greet him!" The wise bridesmaids refilled their lamps and went to meet him, but the lamps of the foolish girls had gone out, and they had to go off to buy more oil. When they returned, the bridegroom and the five bridesmaids had already gone into the wedding hall.'

Discussion

Has anyone ever been a bridesmaid or a page at a wedding?

What did you wear and what did you do?

In the parable, who were the ten bridesmaids waiting for?

They were waiting to greet the bridegroom when he arrived, and to show him the way to the wedding hall. The bridegroom and bride are the ones who are getting married, becoming man and wife, so he is a very special person at the wedding.

Did they know when he would arrive?

They knew that he was coming, but they did not know the exact time he would arrive.

Why were the wise bridesmaids ready for his coming and the foolish bridesmaids not?

The five sensible girls knew that the bridegroom could arrive at any time – day or night! They brought flasks of oil for their lamps, in case the bridegroom was late, and their lamps had burned low. The foolish bridesmaids did not think ahead and brought no extra oil for their lamps. When the bridegroom suddenly arrived, they were not ready to meet him, and by the time they had filled their lamps, the bridegroom had already come and gone.

Jesus uses parables to give us a message. What do you think today's message is?

Jesus uses this story to tell us that we must always *be ready*. Like the bridesmaids, we know that Jesus will come again, but we do not know the exact day or time. The wise bridesmaids kept themselves ready so that they were not taken by surprise when the bridegroom finally arrived.

How can we keep ourselves ready for when Jesus returns?

If we can live each day as well as possible, and make each day our best, then we will always be ready to greet Jesus when he comes. By trying to be good and to live as Jesus taught us, ready to say sorry when we get things wrong and to forgive others, then we will be like the wise bridesmaids who kept their lamps burning, and be ready for Jesus when he comes.

Activity

Make the moving models of the lamp as shown. You may find it helpful to photocopy onto thin card.

Closing Prayer

Lord Jesus,
we know that one day you will return
and we will be with you in heaven.
Help us to make each day our best,
so that we will always be ready
to greet you.

'Be ready'
'Be ready'

Gifts from God

Listening

(cf Matthew 25:14-30)

One day Jesus said, 'Once there were three men who had each been given different numbers of talents. The first man had five, the second man, three and the third, one. They were free to use these talents however they wished. The first man used his talents well and did a lot of good with them; the second man also worked hard and used what he had been given wisely, but the third man felt that he had little to offer, so he hid his talent away from everyone and did not use it. The time came to meet the one who had given each of them their talents, and they told him in turn how they had used them. He was very pleased with the first and second men, but not with the third man who had wasted what he had been given.'

Talking

If we say that someone has a talent, what do we mean?

We mean that they have a special gift or skill for doing something.

In the story Jesus told, each man was given a number of talents. Who gives us our talents?

Any gifts or talents we have, have been given to us by God our Father.

Tell me about some of the talents which God has given to each of you. – Encourage the children to talk about one thing which they do well, for example:

- swimming
- making people laugh
- singing
- dancing
- playing a musical instrument
- drawing
- reading

In the story can you remember what the men did with their talents?

Two of them used their talents well and did a lot of good with them. The other man kept his talent hidden from everyone and did not share it.

What does God want us to do with the talents he has given us?

When someone gives us a present, they love to see us using it and getting pleasure from it. Our talents are gifts from God, given to us because he loves us. They are very precious and must not be wasted, but instead be put to good use.

Doing

Cut out a variety of parcel shapes or use some small boxes – enough for more than one each, and ask the children to colour them or wrap them so that they look like gift boxes. Then give each child a label on which to write one of their own talents before attaching it to a box. These can be pinned to a board with the caption 'Our gifts from God'.

Praying

Heavenly Father, we thank you for the talents
which you have given to each of us.
Whatever our gifts may be,
teach us to use them wisely,
and for the good of others.

THE SHEPHERD AND HIS FLOCK

READING

(cf Mark 6:30-34)

After preaching to the people and curing many that were sick, the apostles returned to Jesus, and told him everything that they had said and done. As usual, crowds of people had followed them; the apostles were feeling tired and in need of a rest. Jesus said to them, 'We will go somewhere quiet and spend some time alone.'

However when Jesus and his friends arrived, a crowd of people had already gathered to meet them. When Jesus saw them, he was filled with pity, because they were like sheep without a shepherd to care for them. He sat down on the hillside and began to teach them.

DISCUSSION

Where had the apostles been?

Jesus had sent them out to the villages to preach his message and heal the sick.

When they returned to Jesus, what did they find?

Wherever Jesus travelled, news soon reached the local people, and it was not long before a crowd of people flocked around him. The apostles were tired after their journeys and eager to spend time telling Jesus about everything that had happened. Jesus was surrounded by people wanting his attention.

What did Jesus suggest that they do?

Jesus suggested that they sail off to find some peace and quiet.

Things did not go quite as planned! What did they find when they moored their boat?

People had guessed their plan and when they arrived a crowd had already gathered.

What did Jesus do?

Did he grow impatient or angry?

Jesus felt a deep sense of love for his followers, and as always, put their needs before his own. The 'good shepherd' knew that these people were his flock. They relied on him to guide and look after them, just as a good shepherd guides and looks after his sheep. He would never let them down or turn them away.

ACTIVITY

Copy the adaptation of *Psalm 23* on to a large sheet of paper. Cut out a 'Good Shepherd' figure and enough sheep for each child. Use these to decorate the words of the prayer and encourage the children to illustrate the picture by drawing tufts of green grass, pools of water, a path etc. Alternatively hand out the colouring-in picture.

CLOSING PRAYER

Read *Psalm 23* aloud together and discuss the words and illustrations with the children.

Psalm 23
The Good Shepherd takes care of all my needs:
He leads me to lush green meadows
and crystal clear pools.
He guides and protects me
and I grow strong in his care.
When night falls, I am not afraid,
for he is always beside me
to protect me from harm.
When he calls, I will follow,
knowing that his love for me
will last forever.

The good Shepherd takes care of all my needs. He leads me to lush green meadows and crystal clear pools. He guides and protects me and I grow strong in his care. When night falls, I am not afraid, for he is always beside me to protect me from harm. When he calls, I will follow, knowing that his love for me will last forever.

THE CAMEL AND THE NEEDLE

LISTENING

(cf Mark 10:17-25)

A man came to Jesus and asked, 'Master, what must I do if I want to go to heaven?'

Jesus said, 'First, you must obey all of God's commandments.'

'I have always tried to live according to the rules of God,' the man said. Jesus looked at the man kindly, and saw his goodness and love. 'Then you must sell everything you own, and give all your money away. By doing this you will have riches in heaven, instead of here on earth.'

The man left Jesus sadly, because he was a very wealthy man. Jesus said to his friends, 'It is easier for a camel to pass through the eye of a needle, than for a rich man to enter the kingdom of heaven!'

TALKING

What did the man want Jesus to tell him?

The man wanted to know what to do to make sure that he would go to heaven when he died.

What answer did Jesus give?

First, Jesus told the man that he must obey God's commandments. Then Jesus told the man that he must give away all his money and everything he owned.

How did the man feel when he heard the words of Jesus?

The man went away feeling sad, because he did not want to give away his riches. Everything he owned meant more to him than the message of Jesus.

Jesus said that it was easier for a camel to pass through the eye of a needle than for a rich man to enter the kingdom of Heaven.

Has anyone ever seen a camel?

How big are they?

How big is a needle?

What do we mean by the eye of the needle?

If you imagine how difficult it would be, for a large camel to climb through a needle, then you can understand what Jesus was trying to tell us!

Why did Jesus want the man to give up what he owned?

He wanted the man to understand that it is more important to have riches in heaven than riches on earth. Money can often make people greedy and selfish, and forgetful about the needs of others. God measures our wealth by our goodness, and whether we are generous and loving, and prepared to share what we have with others.

DOING

Photocopy the illustration. Give one of each to every child, and after colouring, help them to make a mobile.

PRAYING

Lord, you see and remember
every act of kindness and generosity
and store them in your heart.
Help us to store up our treasure in heaven,
so that we can share everlasting life with you
at the end of time.

Gold

The generous woman

Listening

(cf Mark 12:41-44)

When Jesus was in the Temple one day, he watched the people putting their money in a collection box as their offering. Many of the wealthy gave large amounts of money. Then a poor old woman came into the Temple, and dropped two small coins, worth as little as one penny, into the box. Seeing this, Jesus turned to his disciples and said, 'This old woman has given more than any of the others! They gave money that they could spare, but she has given *all* the money that she had.'

Talking

Do you mind sharing what you have with other people?

It is easy to share when we have plenty, because we do not really miss what we have given away. It is much harder to give to others when we have very little ourselves.

Imagine you have a large bag of sweets, and were asked to share it with everyone in this room. Would you find it hard to do?

Probably not, because there would be enough to give everyone a sweet, and still have plenty left.

Now imagine you had just one of your favourite sweets! How easy do you think it would be to give that precious sweet away to someone else?

What did Jesus say about the rich men?

The rich men had plenty of money and, like the large bag of sweets, it made little difference to them if they gave lots of it away.

The poor old woman only gave two small coins, and yet Jesus said that she had given the most. Why?

The old woman gave very little, but it was *all* she had, so she had given everything.

What message does today's reading have for us?

Today's reading teaches us about giving and sharing. It is not *how much* we give that is important, but *how* we give it, and what is in our hearts when we share something. Giving and sharing with a loving and sincere heart is what really matters to God.

What can you give and share with other people? – (Encourage the children to suggest their own ideas.)

- your love
- your time
- your toys and possessions
- your happiness
- your friendship

Doing

Photocopy this picture showing the old widow putting all that she had into the offerings box. Encourage the children to draw Jesus and some rich men as part of the scene.

Praying

Dear Lord, teach us how to share
and never to be greedy,
because everything that we have
comes from you.

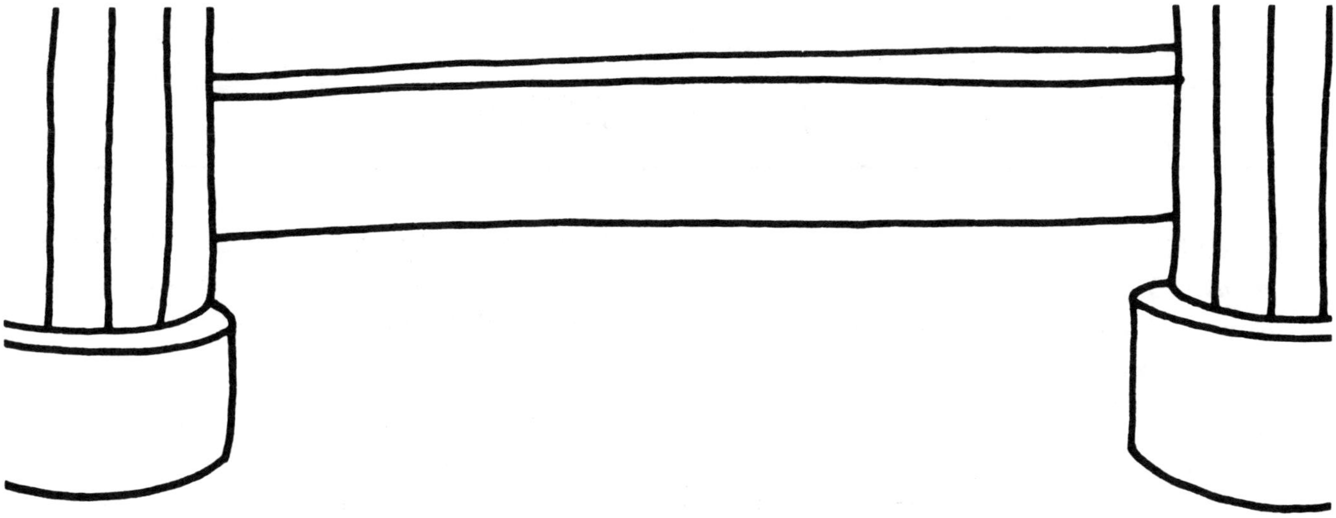

Jesus is Born

Reading

(cf Luke 2:1-20)

Joseph and Mary arrived in Bethlehem to register for the census ordered by the Roman Emperor Augustus. The time came for Mary to have her baby, and he was born in a stable, because there was no room at the inn. She wrapped him in strips of cloth and laid him in a manger. On a hillside near the town, some shepherds were watching over their sheep. Suddenly, an angel appeared and the sky was filled with God's glory. The shepherds were terrified, but the angel said, 'Do not be afraid, for I have great news for you. Today a baby has been born in Bethlehem. He is Christ the Lord. You will find him lying in a manger.' The sky was filled with the sound of angels singing, 'Glory to God in the highest, and peace to all people on earth!' The shepherds hurried to Bethlehem and soon found the stable. There in the manger lay a tiny baby. They told Mary and Joseph what they had seen and heard that night, and they shared their amazement. Mary listened carefully and cherished all these things in her heart. The shepherds went back to their sheep on the hillside, singing God's praises, for everything had been as the angel had said.

Discussion

Use a prepared christingle as a visual aid for the discussion and ask the children if they know what the different parts of the christingle symbolise.

The christingle comprises:

1. An orange – this represents our world.
2. A candle pushed into the top – this represents the 'light' of the world.
3. A red ribbon around the orange – this represents the blood of Christ.
4. Four cocktail sticks with dried fruit stuck on – these represent the fruits of the earth, and the abundance of the four seasons.

The points to emphasise are:

1. That Jesus came to save the whole world and everyone in it.
2. His light reaches out to all people.
3. By dying on the cross, he shed his blood and saved us all from our sins.
4. God is generous and gave us all a wonderful world, with plenty of food and resources. We should not be greedy, and must always try to share what we can with others. This is very appropriate to remember at Christmas.

Activity

Help each child to make a christingle. Much of the preparation can be done in advance (they can be lit at home!) Afterwards sing carols with the children.

If plenty of notice is given, the children can bring non-perishable foodstuffs in to make up a hamper to be given to a worthy cause.

Closing Prayer

Dear Lord Jesus,
on this Christmas morning,
fill us with the joy and wonder
which the shepherds shared with Mary and Joseph.
May our hearts and our homes
be filled with the peace and love
you shared with the world.

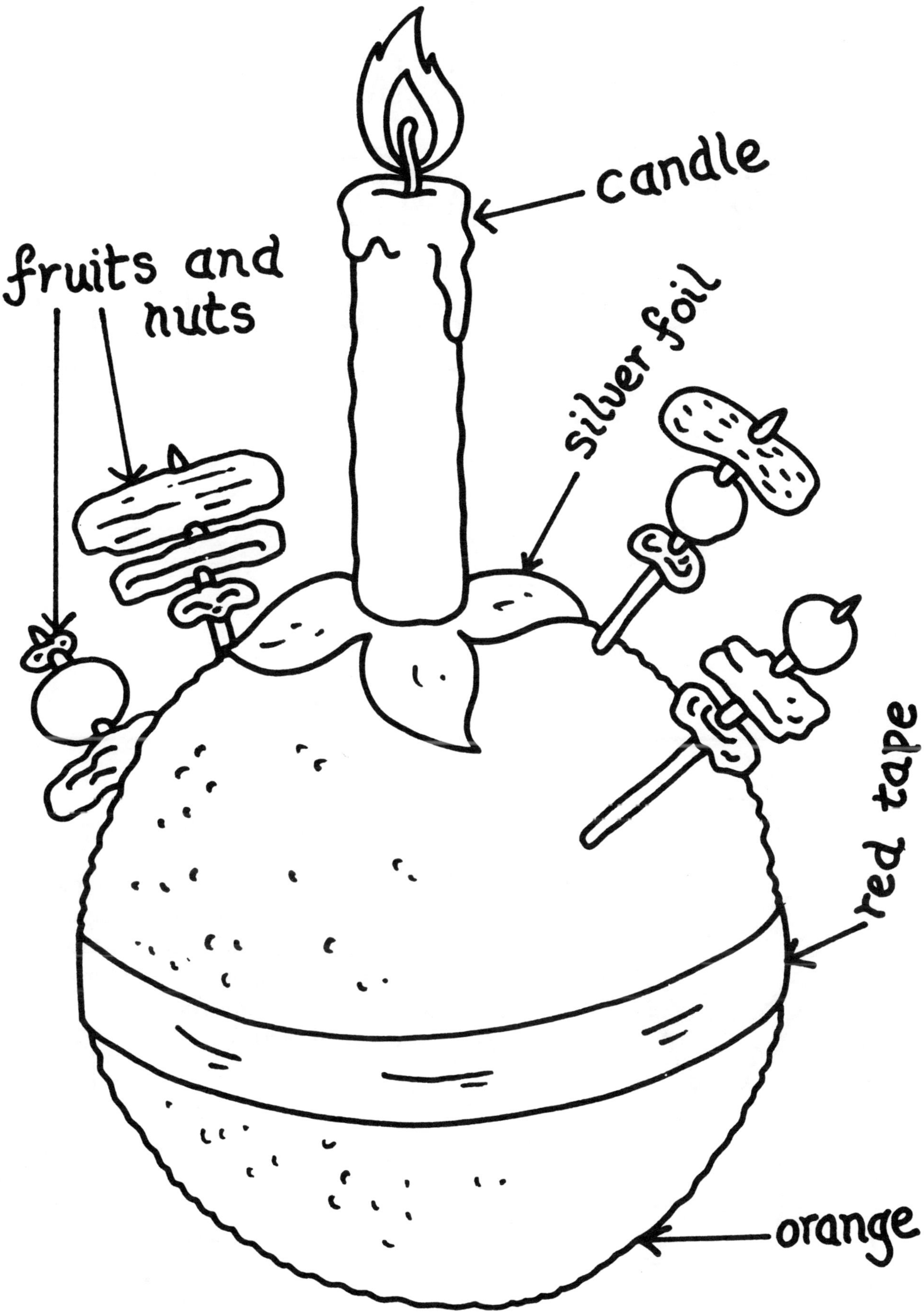
candle
fruits and nuts
silver foil
red tape
orange

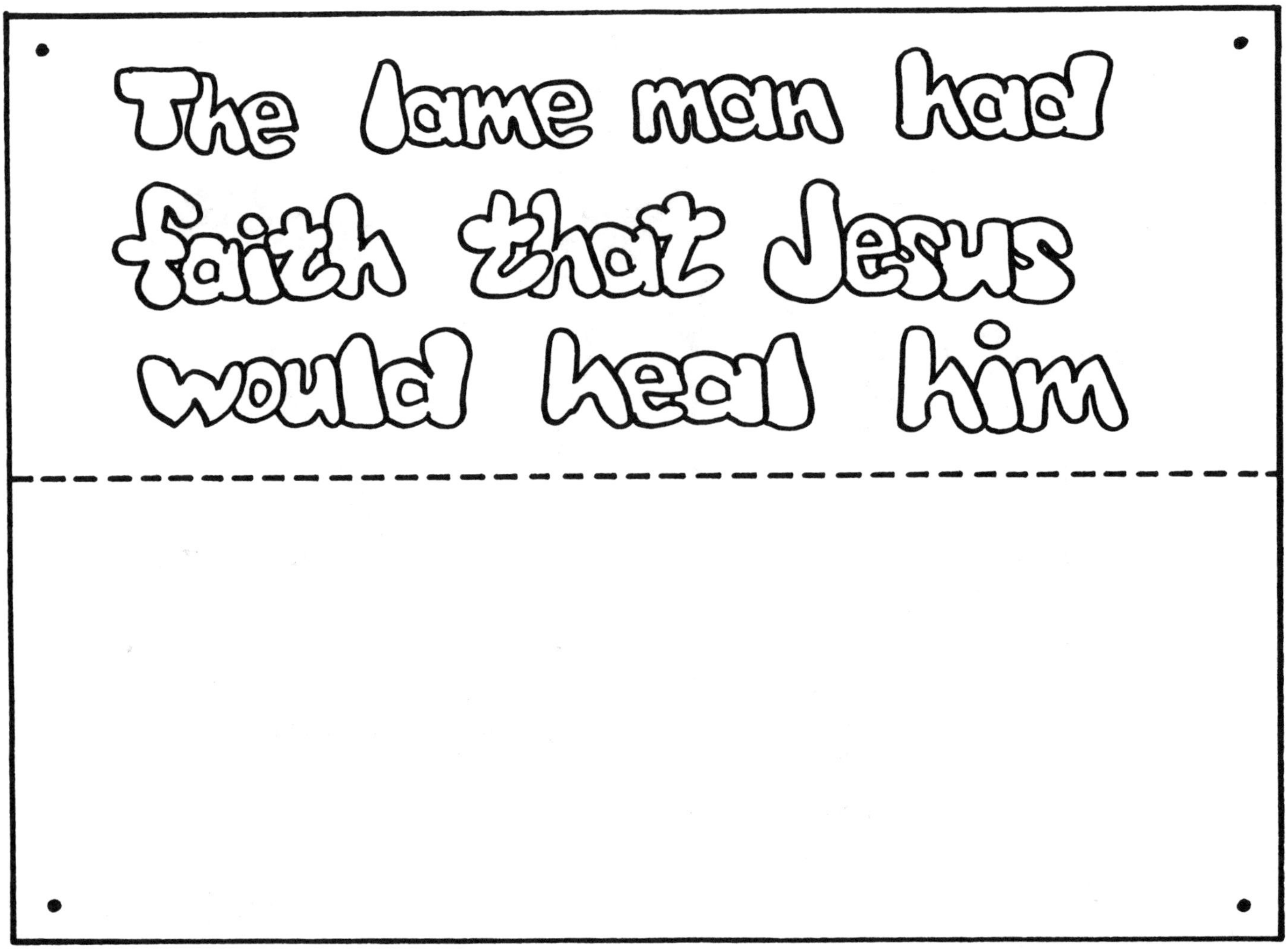

1. Photocopy onto thin card.
2. Colour and cut out.
3. Fold rectangle outwards on dotted line.
4. Pierce holes on four dots marked at corners and thread strings through.
5. Put man inside – as if his four friends were about to let him down through the roof.
6. Hang up in your room by the threads.

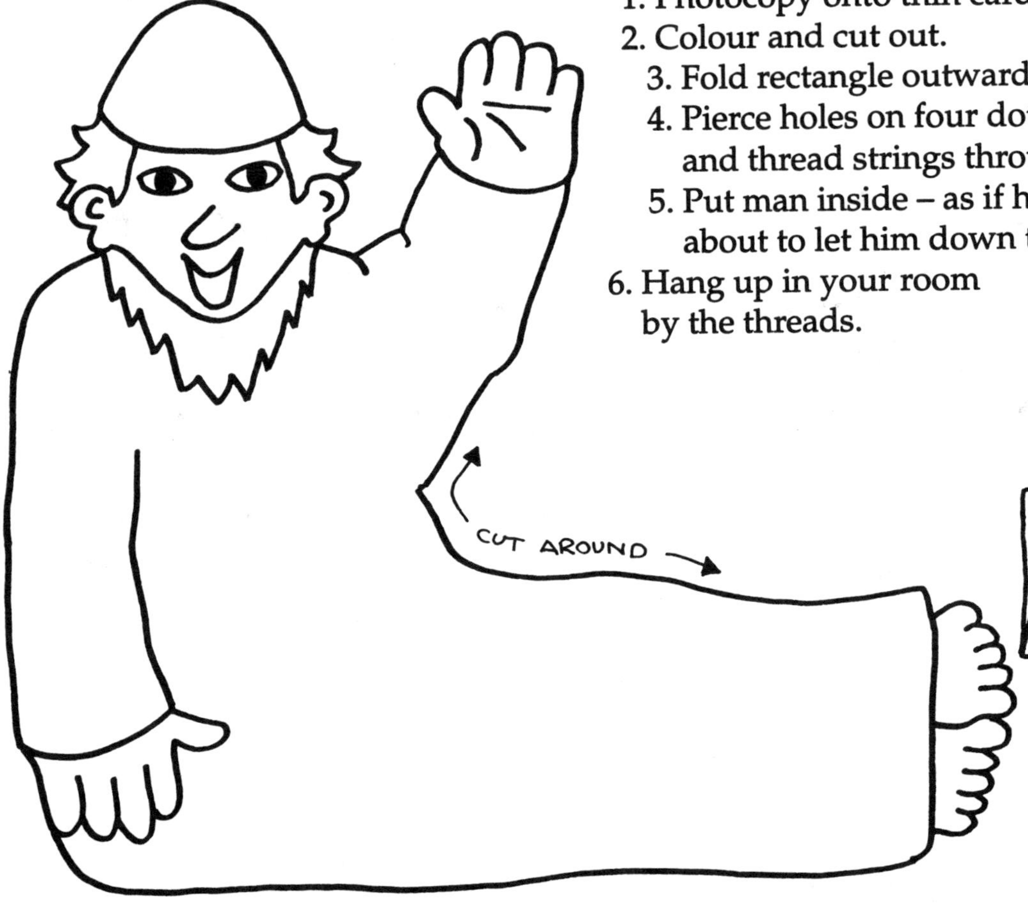

1. Photocopy onto thin card. 2. Colour and cut out.
3. Cut off long thin strip with dot B marked on it.
4. Fold picture inwards on dotted lines _ . _ . _ .
5. Cut slit XY. 6. Pierce dots A and B and attach with paper fastener through A, then through **slit**, then B.

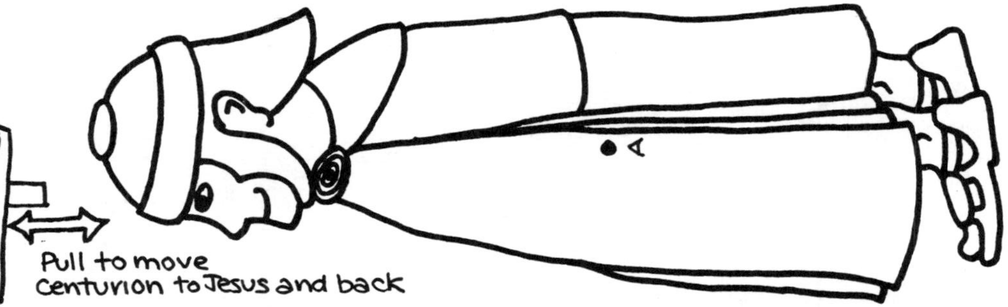

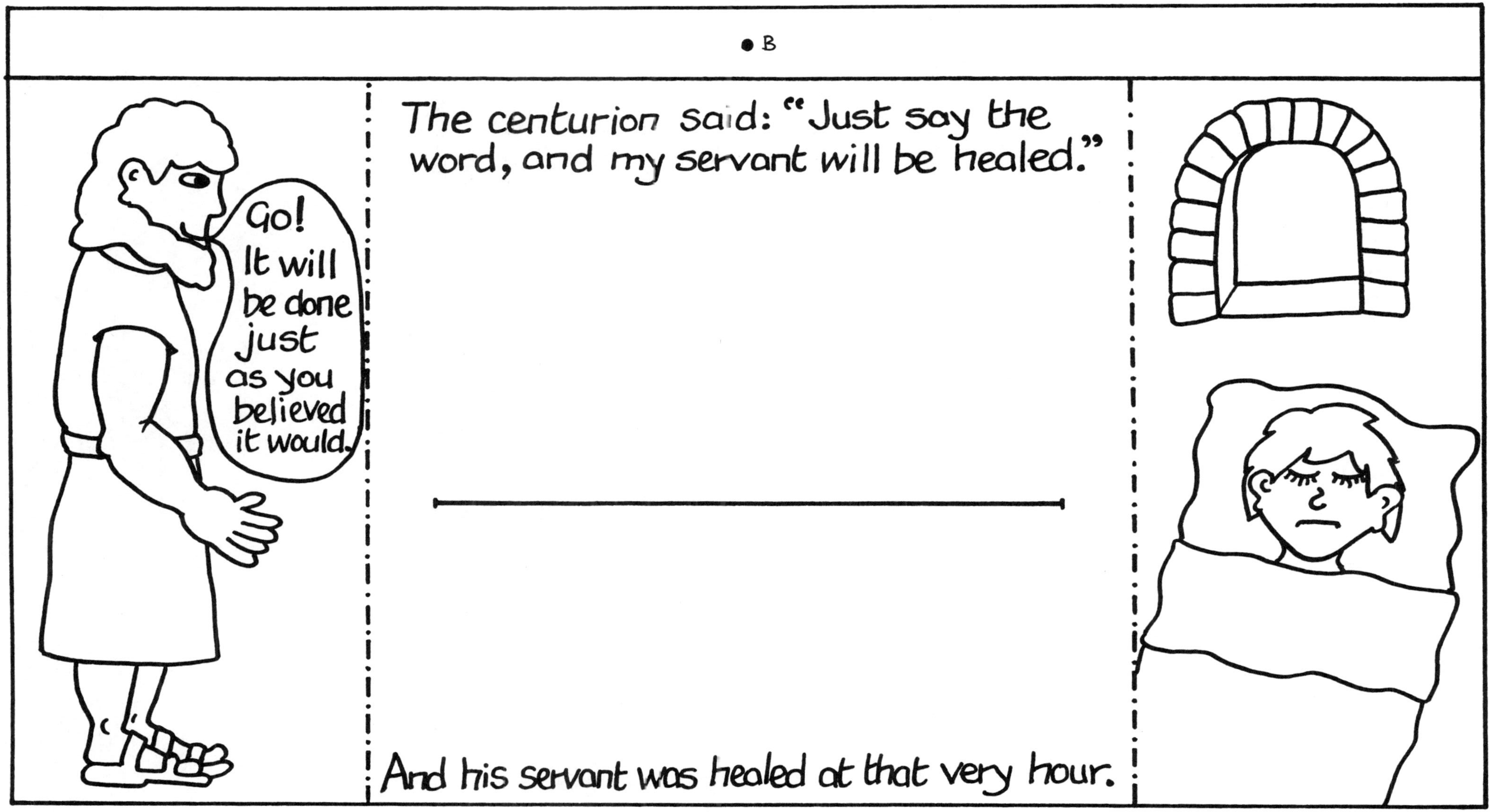

Good fruit

Reading

(cf Luke 6:43-45)

One day Jesus told this parable, 'Fruit that is rotten and bad can never grow on a strong and healthy tree, just as good fruit cannot grow on a tree that is sick and diseased.

'Different fruits grow on different trees, and everyone knows which fruit belongs to which type of tree. Like the tree and its fruit, the good will speak and act kindly, because of the goodness in their hearts.'

Discussion

Does anyone have a fruit tree growing in their garden?

What type of tree is it?

What is the easiest way to tell the difference between an apple and a pear tree?

At certain times of the year, trees can be identified by the fruit growing on their branches. Apples only grow on apple trees, and pears only grow on pear trees!

(Show the children some pictures of different fruit trees and their fruit; a good gardening book should provide these.)

What do you need to get a good crop of tasty healthy apples?

An apple tree that is healthy and well cared for will usually produce lots of good fruit. A tree which is attacked by disease or pests, or whose branches and trunk become rotten, will produce only a few poor apples.

What is the message of today's parable?

Just as you can tell whether a tree is good or bad by the fruit it grows, so the words and actions of people reveal the state of their hearts. If we are healthy and strong, and full of God's goodness, then that goodness will show in our lives. If our hearts are selfish and unkind, then we will be selfish and unkind to people.

How can we make sure our lives are filled with God's love and goodness?

God comes to each one of us in a very special way when we receive the Holy Spirit. Just as a tree needs to be nourished to produce good fruit, so we need the Holy Spirit to nourish us. We invite Jesus into our lives and the goodness he shares with us overflows into our daily words and actions.

Activity

The children can cut out the good apples and stick them in the tree. Help them to assemble the pictures on a background after they have been coloured, and add the caption: 'The Fruits of Goodness'.

Closing Prayer

Lord Jesus,
may people see the fuits of your love
and goodness in our words
and the way we treat other people.

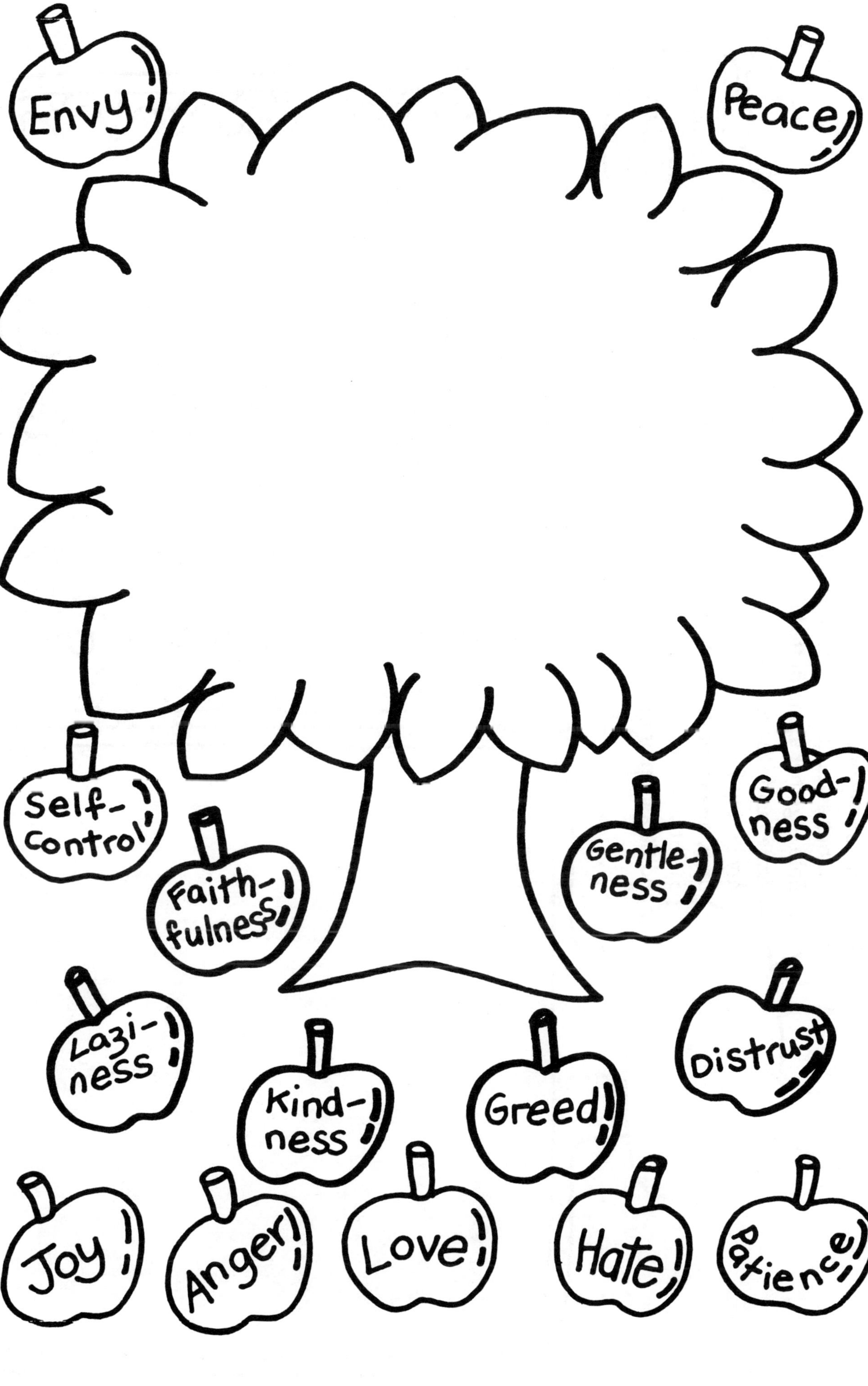
Envy
Peace
Self-control
Good-ness
Gentle-ness
Faith-fulness
Lazi-ness
Distrust
Kind-ness
Greed
Joy
Anger
Love
Hate
Patience

1. Photocopy onto thin card.
2. Colour and cut out – draw pattern on back.
3. Fold together along dotted line _ _ _ .
4. Write inside the words 'I will give my best to Jesus – time, money, effort'
5. Cut small hole in top of bottle and tie a loop of ribbon through it.

1. Photocopy onto thin card.
2. Colour and cut out.
3. Pierce dots A and B and attach A in front of B using a paper fastener.
4. Fold covers inwards on dotted line _ . _ . _ . then glue **behind** end beyond foldline and attach to end of bed.
5. Put Jairus' daughter lying down with cover over top.
6. Lift up cover and turn girl to stand up out of bed.

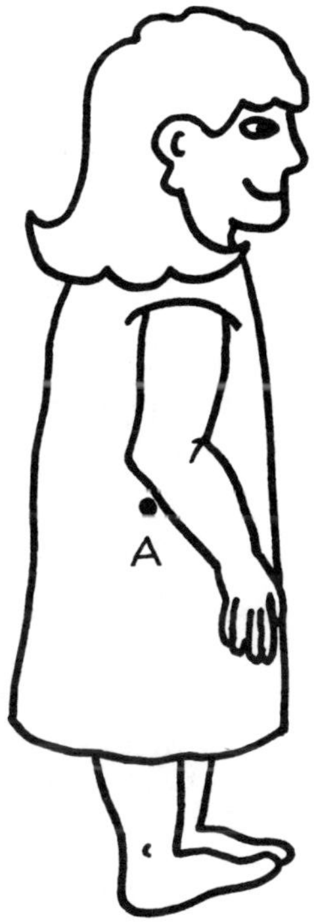

Jesus took her by the hand and said: "My child, get up!" Her spirit returned, and at once she stood up. Then Jesus told them to give her something to eat.
Luke 6:54-55

MAKE TIME TO LISTEN

LISTENING

(cf Luke 10:38-42)

One day Jesus and his disciples came to the village called Bethany where his friends Martha and Mary lived. They welcomed Jesus and his followers and invited them to stay for a meal.

While Martha busied herself preparing and serving the food, her sister Mary sat calmly beside Jesus and listened to him talking. Martha worked hard, and all the while Mary sat and listened to Jesus. Finally Martha got upset and said to Jesus, 'Lord must I do all this work on my own? Tell Mary to come and help me!'

'Martha, Martha,' Jesus said. 'Do not let these things upset you; they are not important. Mary has chosen to listen to me and that is the most important thing of all.'

TALKING

Martha was very busy and had a lot to do. What do you imagine she had to do?

Jesus and his disciples had been invited to stay for a meal, so Martha had to prepare a lot of food. The travellers were thirsty after their journey, and Martha had to organise drinks for everyone.

What did Mary do while Martha was so busy?

Mary sat down beside Jesus and simply listened to his words.

How did Martha feel about this?

Martha became angry with Mary, perhaps because she thought that she was being lazy, leaving her to do all the work. Martha may also have felt a little jealous of her sister, because she too wanted to sit at Jesus' feet and listen to him.

What did Jesus say when Martha complained?

Jesus told Martha that Mary had chosen to do the right thing. He was grateful for all the work that Martha had done for them, but what really made him happy was making time to listen to the word of God; nothing was more important!

What does this story teach us?

We all lead hectic and busy lives, and sometimes we forget what is really important: to make time for Jesus in our lives and to listen as he speaks to us.

DOING

Ask each child to draw a picture of themselves listening to God's word at Church, or making time for Jesus as they say their prayers.

PRAYING

Lord Jesus, we pray that we will
always make you welcome
and be ready to spend time
listening to your Word.

Making Time For Jesus

LISTENING TO GOD'S WORD AT CHURCH

TALKING TO GOD AT PRAYERTIME

1. Photocopy onto thin card.
2. Colour in and cut round **outer** rectangle – cut out foods.
3. Fold **outwards** on _ . _ . _ lines and **inwards** on _ _ _ lines.
4. Through all four thicknesses of card, cut outline of man's head and shoulders.
5. Draw faces on other three people and colour in.
6. Stick foods on table. 7. Reverse the zig-zag folds and stand up.

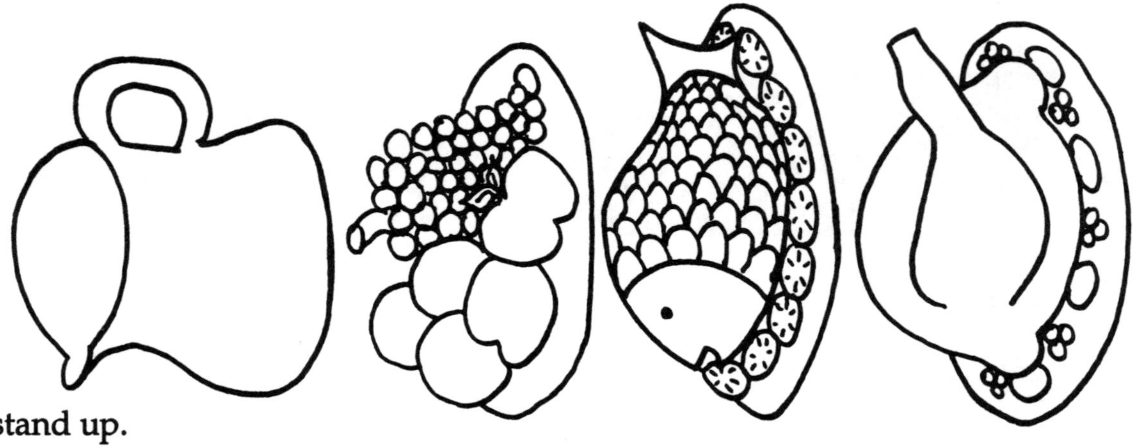

1. Photocopy onto thin card. 2. Cut out.
3. Join back and front of sheep using a cork fastened on with Blu-tack or sticky fixers – make sure feet are level before sticking. (Corks available from winemaking suppliers.)
4. You could play a 'lost sheep' game – everyone goes out of the room while one person hides the sheep. See who can find the 'lost sheep'.

33 JESUS' PARABLES 2 – THE TWO HOUSES Matthew 7:24-27

1. Photocopy onto thin card.
2. Colour in and cut out.
3. Sellotape a safety pin onto the back to make a badge.

ALWAYS BE HONEST

READING

(cf Luke 16:10-11)

Jesus said, 'When a person is honest about the small things in life, then they will be honest about more important things too. If you cannot be trusted with something as unimportant as money, how can you be trusted with the most precious treasure of all?'

DISCUSSION

If you saw someone dropping a pound coin without noticing, what would you do?

You would have to choose between being honest, and giving the coin back, or dishonest, and keeping the coin yourself. When a person is filled with the spirit of God's goodness, they can be trusted to make the right choice. A good person will always be honest, however great or small the amount of money may be.

Listen to this short story:

Peter had been saving his pocket money for a long time and just needed one more pound to afford the football he wanted so much. One day while shopping with his mum, he noticed that an old lady had dropped some money as she struggled to put it in her purse. The coin rolled across the floor and lay unnoticed. Peter picked it up and found to his delight that it was a pound, just what he needed! (At this point ask the children what they think Peter should do, before reading on to see if they were right!)

. . . Peter took the coin over to the old woman who thanked him for his kindness and honesty. Peter smiled, feeling very good inside.

Why do you think Peter felt good inside? – Peter had chosen God's way, by being honest and truthful. His actions had made the old woman very happy, and seeing her happiness made him feel good inside. We all know how wonderful we feel when we show someone that we care about them. Peter felt the joy of sharing God's love and knowing that God was pleased with him.

What is the most precious treasure of all which Jesus trusts us with?

The most precious treasure of all is the love of our heavenly Father which means more than all our worldly possessions. Money cannot make us happy, because true happiness comes from loving God. We are free to live as we choose, because God trusts us to do what we know is right.

ACTIVITY

Either use the activity sheets or help each child to fold a sheet of paper in half to find the middle. On one half, ask them to draw a picture of themselves in the playground, with a £1 coin they have found at their feet. Give each child a 'choice wheel' and a butterfly pin and help them to pin it on the other half of the paper. Get the children to draw an arrow and, turning the wheel, to point to whatever choice they think they should make. Discuss!

CLOSING PRAYER

Lord, help us to be truthful and honest with each other and to be guided by your goodness.

"Be Honest"

Tell no-one
Put it in my pocket
Take it to my teacher
Buy some sweets
Turn
Turn

THANK YOU, JESUS

LISTENING

(cf Luke 17:12-19)

On the way to Jerusalem, Jesus drew near a village where he found ten lepers waiting to meet him. Keeping their distance they called out to him, 'Jesus of Nazareth, have pity and help us!'

Jesus saw their suffering and said, 'Go and show yourselves to the priest.'

They set off to see the priest and on the way they realised that their leprosy had disappeared and they were cured! As the others ran to find the priest, one of the ten went back to find Jesus. He threw himself down before him, praising God and thanking Jesus for his kindness. 'Were the others not cured too?' Jesus asked. 'Yet only one has bothered to thank God for his goodness.' Then he said to the man, 'Now go and see the priest. Your faith in God has made you well.'

TALKING

In what ways did lepers suffer?

They suffered from the disease of leprosy which causes deformity with the loss of limbs and sometimes blindness. They also suffered because they were driven away from their homes and families, to live far away from villages and towns. They had to warn people that they were 'unclean' by ringing a bell or shouting, because everyone was afraid of catching their disease. Their lives were miserable and their suffering was very great.

What did Jesus do when they asked for his help?

Jesus took pity on them and told them to go and show themselves to the priest. The priest was the person who decided whether their leprosy had gone and gave them permission to live with their families again. They showed how much they believed in Jesus because they set off at once, and trusted him to cure them.

What did one of the lepers do when he realised that he had been cured?

He remembered to go back to Jesus and say thank you. The others had rushed off to see the priest and be reunited with their families and friends again.

Do you think that Jesus was pleased that one said 'thank you'?

Jesus was very pleased with the one leper who had remembered to say thank you but was disappointed that the other nine did not. People often forget to thank Jesus when something good happens. All too often we take things for granted and forget to thank God for all his kindness.

DOING

Photocopy the picture onto some stiff paper to make a card. Fold a 4cm wide strip of paper and stick one end inside the card, and the other end onto the 'Thank you Jesus' badge. Encourage the children to write something that *they* want to thank Jesus for or write it for them.

PRAYING

Lord Jesus, the lepers asked for your help
and you gave them new life and new hope.
Thank you for all the love
and kindness you give to us.

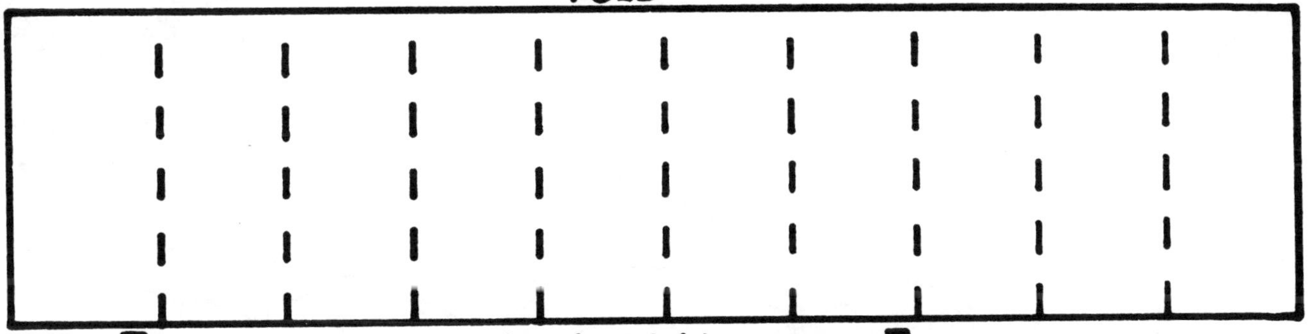

Fold along dotted lines first one way then the other

Thankyou Jesus for

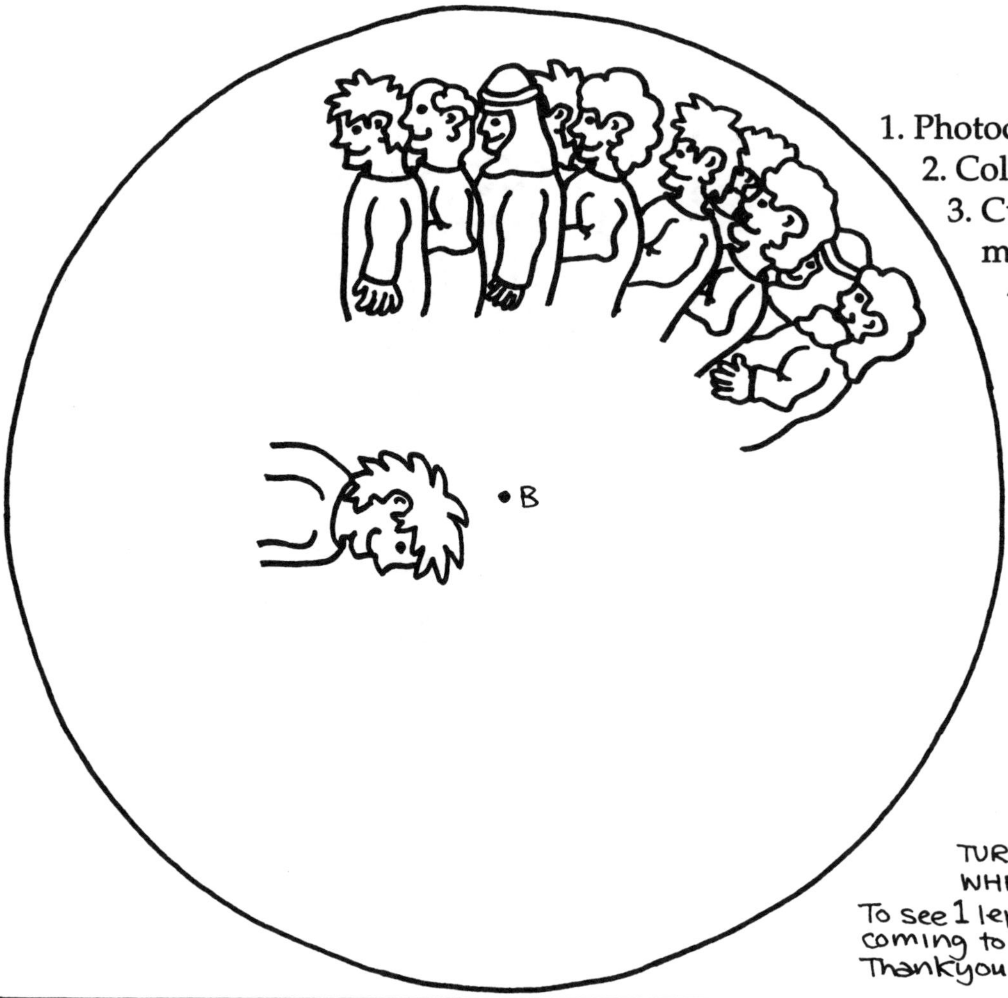

1. Photocopy onto thin card.
2. Colour and cut out.
3. Cut out two windows in main picture.
4. Pierce dots A and B and attach B behind A using a paper fastener.
5. Turn wheel to see ten lepers going away healed to show the priests, then only one leper coming back to Jesus to say 'thank you'.

1. Photocopy onto thin card. 2. Colour in. Cut around **rectangle** with tree on and cut out all four Zacchaeus figures.
3. Fold tree strip along dotted lines zig-zag fashion, outwards on lines _ _ _ and inwards on lines _ . _ . _ .
4. Cut along tree outline through **all four** thicknesses of card.
5. Position four Zacchaeus figures as indicated below: –

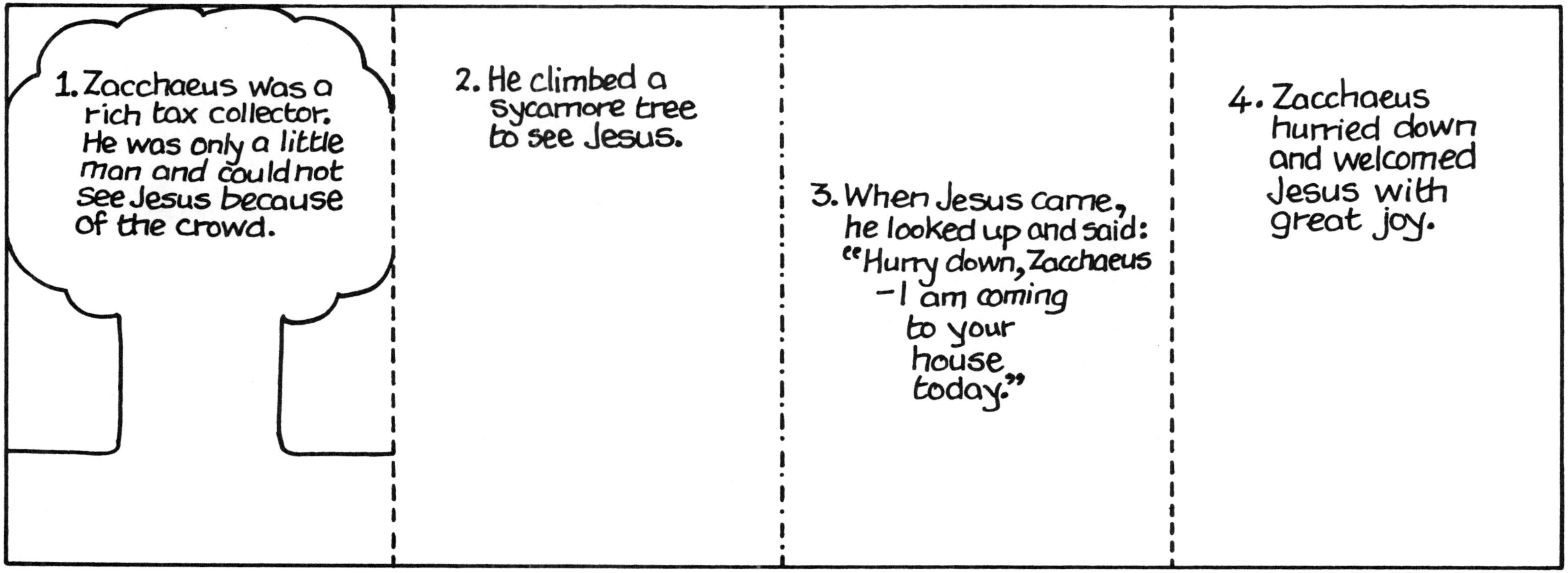

THE STORY OF ZACCHAEUS

LISTENING

(cf Luke 19:1-10)

Jesus went to a town called Jericho, where a man called Zacchaeus lived. Nobody liked Zacchaeus because he was a tax collector who cheated people to make himself rich. When Jesus arrived, crowds gathered to see him and Zacchaeus was among them. Zacchaeus was very small and could not see Jesus because of the crowds, so he climbed a tree to get a better view. As Jesus passed by, he looked up and said, 'Come down Zacchaeus! I want to visit your house today.'

Zacchaeus almost fell out of the tree with surprise. Hearing this, the crowd began to grumble and complain. 'How can Jesus speak to such a wicked man!' they said.

Then Zacchaeus turned to Jesus and said, 'Lord, I know that I am dishonest, but I want to change and put things right! I will give half of everything I own to the poor, and pay back everything I have stolen four times over.' Jesus smiled at Zacchaeus and said, 'I have come to find and save anyone who has lost their way. Now change your heart and make a fresh start.'

TALKING

Why did the people think that Zacchaeus was wicked?

Zacchaeus was the chief tax collector in Jericho. Tax collectors grew rich by charging extra taxes and cheating the people out of their money.

Why did Zacchaeus end up sitting in a tree?

Zacchaeus was a very short man, and could not see Jesus because of the crowds around him. Zacchaeus climbed the tree to get a good view.

What did Jesus do as he walked by?

Jesus called Zacchaeus to come down and take him to his home.

The crowds, and Zacchaeus himself, were shocked when Jesus did this. Why were they so surprised?

The crowds did not think that Jesus should have anything to do with such a dishonest man. None of them liked Zacchaeus, and he had no friends until Jesus offered his friendship. Jesus was willing to forgive and forget what Zacchaeus had done, and to give him the chance to make a fresh start.

Jesus came to call all of us back to God's love and away from selfishness and greed. What did Zacchaeus promise to do to show that he had truly had a change of heart?

He promised to be generous and to give back everything he owed and more. Jesus loved Zacchaeus despite his faults, and because of this love Zacchaeus turned back to God. We all make mistakes and Jesus calls each one of us to turn back to his love, and change our hearts. He is full of forgiveness, and will fill us with his love and goodness to help us make a fresh start.

DOING

Cut out a tree shape with branches and the figure of Zacchaeus. After colouring, place Zacchaeus 'in' the tree and attach it to a sheet of paper. The children can glue on leaves made from tissue paper or real leaves if preferred. Add the caption, 'Zacchaeus finds a friend!'

PRAYING

Lord Jesus, make our heart more loving
and ready to forgive others
just as you forgive us.

Zacchaeus finds a friend!

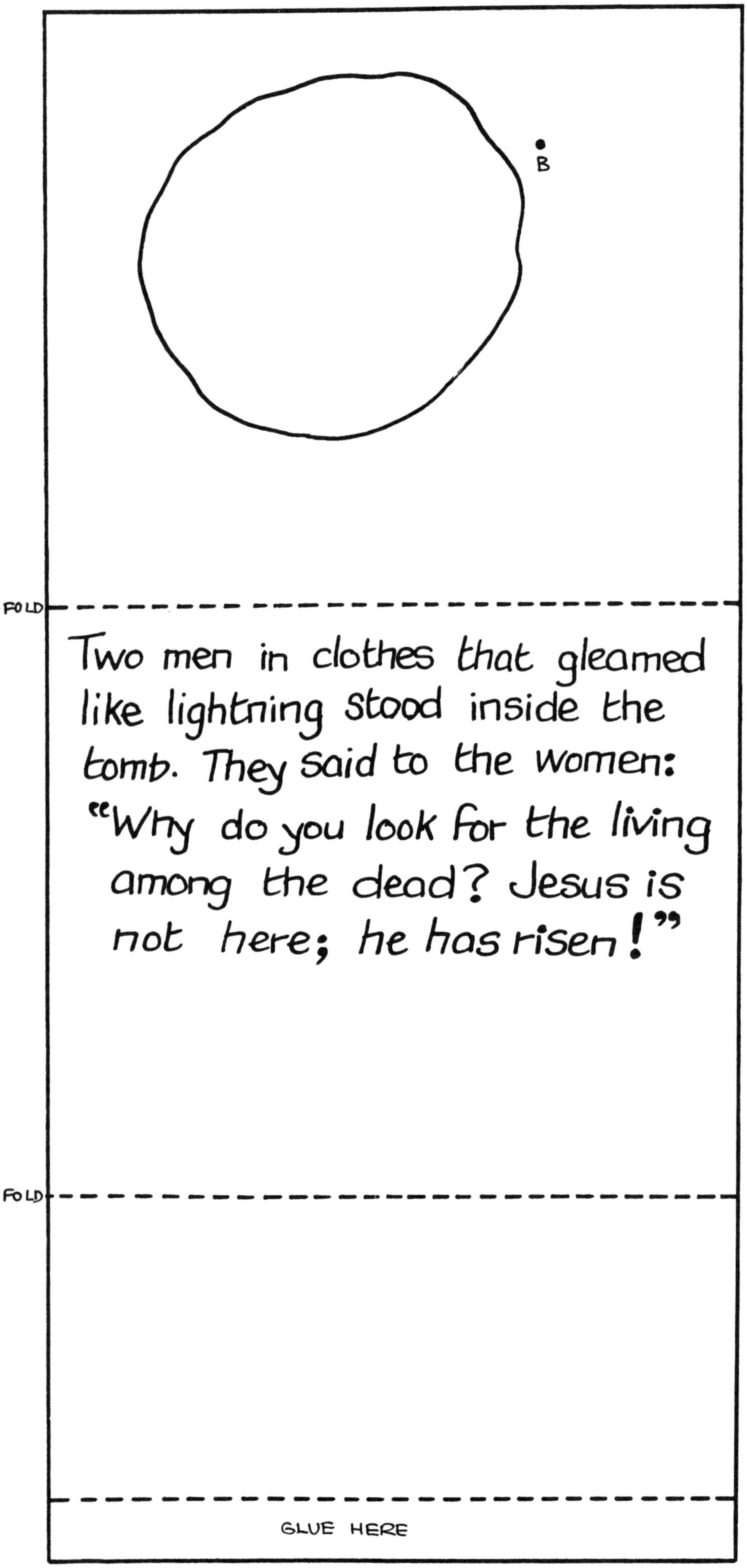

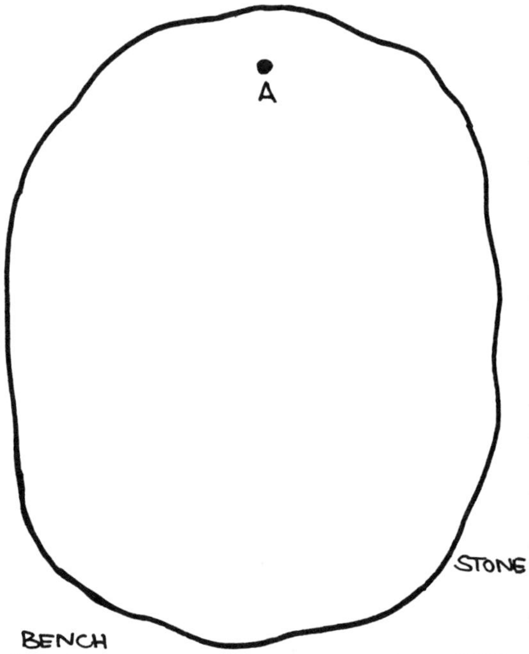

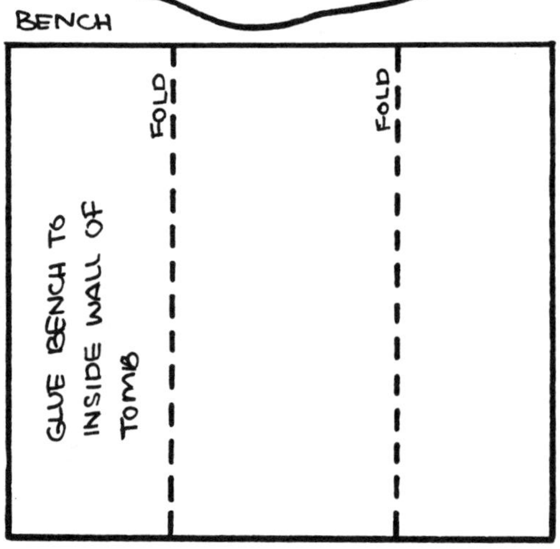

1. Photocopy onto thin card.
2. Colour and cut out.
3. Fold out on all dotted lines.
4. Glue tomb into tent shape.
5. Pierce dots A and B – attach A over B using a paper fastener.
6. Glue folded bench to back inside wall of tomb.
7. Glue angels to front of bench so they can be seen when stone rolled away.

1. Photocopy onto thin card.
2. Colour and cut out – colour circle half blue and half red.
3. Cut out ovals in top of two water jars.
4. Pierce dots A and B and attach B behind A using a paper fastener.
5. Line up wheel so that blue is showing in tops of water jars, then turn wheel to see wine (red) appear in jars.
6. Fill in the right words in spaces.

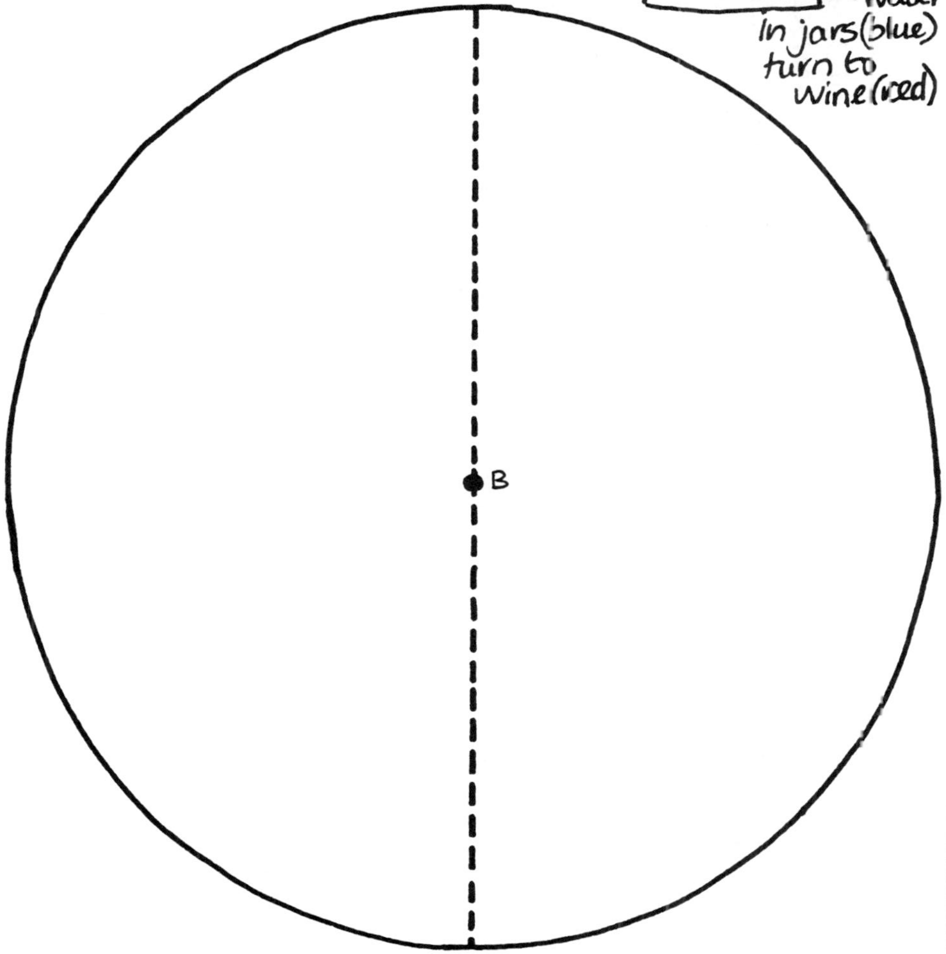

JESUS FEEDS THE PEOPLE

LISTENING

(cf John 6:1-15)

Jesus crossed the Sea of Galilee, and seeing that a large crowd had followed him along the shore, he turned to Philip and asked, 'Where can we buy some bread to feed these people?' Philip answered, 'Master, it would cost a fortune to give each person even a small piece of bread!'

Then a small boy, with five loaves and two fish was brought to Jesus. 'This is all the food we have!' the disciples said.

'Tell the people to sit down,' Jesus said, and taking the bread and fish, he gave thanks to God. Then he gave the food out to as many as five thousand people, and there was plenty for everyone. When they had finished eating, they filled twelve baskets with the scraps that were left! These people saw and believed that Jesus was indeed the Son of God.

TALKING

What did the people on the hillside need that day?

The people had walked many miles that day to be with Jesus, and they were tired and hungry. It was miles to the nearest town, and even then, Jesus and his disciples did not have enough money to buy food for so many! The people needed food, and Jesus provided it for them.

How many people were in the crowd that day?

The Gospel tells us that as many as 5000 people needed to be fed that day. The exact number does not really matter, because normally five loaves and two fish could not possibly feed them all.

Have you ever shared a meal with a large number of people?

At certain times of year, perhaps at Christmas or a birthday party, many friends and relatives gather together to share a meal. Usually a lot of planning and preparation takes place, to make sure that there is enough for everyone to eat and drink. Imagine how the disciples must have felt when Jesus suddenly decided that they should feed this huge crowd of people!

What did Jesus do with the loaves and the fish?

He thanked God for his goodness, blessed the food and then shared it with the people.

Jesus said, 'I am the Bread of Life. If you eat this bread, I will live in you and you in me.' So if we trust in Jesus we can grow in God's love and be filled with joy and goodness.

DOING

Ask each child to draw a picture of a basket and then glue two cut-out fish and five loaves into place on their picture. After colouring, help them to write, 'Jesus feeds his people' on their completed picture.

PRAYING

Lord Jesus, as you fed the hungry crowds,
feed *us* with the bread of life.
Through the gift of yourself
help us to become more like you.

1. Photocopy onto thin card.
2. Colour and cut out.
3. Fold outwards on dotted line _ _ _ .
4. Make five loaves and two fishes from brown and blue paper – stick inside.

1. Photocopy onto thin card.
2. Cut out all shapes and colour in.
3. Colour mud patch brown.
4. Cover pool shape with aluminium foil.
5. Cut out finger holes on finger puppets of Jesus and the blind man.
6. Stick blind face onto blind man using sticky putty.
7. Act out the story of the healing of the blind man using your finger puppets – when man is healed, take off the blind face so he can see!

A GRAIN OF WHEAT

LISTENING

(cf John 12:23-27)

Jesus said to his disciples, 'The time has come for me to be glorified. Just as a grain of wheat must die to produce a harvest of many grains, so the Son of God must die so that many can live.'

Jesus was troubled because he knew the time for him to die was fast approaching.

'I could ask my heavenly Father to stop this thing from happening, but it was for this very reason that I have come,' he said.

TALKING

Why did Jesus feel troubled?

He knew that soon he would be betrayed by Judas and would suffer and die on the cross.

Do you think he was afraid?

No one likes to suffer, and Jesus knew what lay ahead of him. He must have felt afraid, but he did not try to avoid what was to happen. Instead he turned to his father and prayed for strength and courage.

What did Jesus say about the grain of wheat?

The wheat plant produces a seed called a 'grain'. A single grain of wheat can produce a plant with many, many grains. To do this the seed itself must die and give up its own life to produce a tall and strong shoot.

Many other familiar plants produce seeds which die so that they can produce new life. Can you think of any examples?

(Encourage the children to discuss vegetable and flower seeds which might be familiar to them. You could show them beans growing in a jar or cress seedlings which have been planted earlier. Let them look at the seeds which these plants came from.)

Jesus used the image of the grain of wheat to try to explain what would happen to him. Do you understand what he was trying to tell us?

Jesus wanted us to understand that, like that of a seed, his death was necessary, if new life was to be given to many. Jesus gave up his life by dying on the cross so that he could have new and everlasting life which we could share with him.

DOING

Colour the drawings of the various stages of the development of a seed from its beginnings to its final harvest. After the pictures have been coloured, help the children to arrange them in sequence and to discuss how the death of one seed can produce a whole new crop.

PRAYING

Lord Jesus, you willingly gave up your life
so that you could share everlasting life
with everyone.
Thank you for your courage and love
and for dying to save us all.

1
2
3
4

I WILL NOT LEAVE YOU ON YOUR OWN

Reading

(cf John 14:16-20)

One day, Jesus said to his disciples, 'I will not leave you on your own, I will ask my Father to send you a helper who will stay with you always. The Spirit of God will be with you and in you, though others will not be able to see him or know that he is there. He will fill you with wisdom and understanding. Soon the world will not see me again, but you will know that I am truly alive.'

Discussion

Jesus was going to leave his disciples and return to his heavenly Father.

Whom did he promise to send?

A special helper – the Holy Spirit.

What would this helper look like?

Jesus told them, 'Others will not be able to see him or know that he is there.' The Holy Spirit is one of the great mysteries of God. He is invisible, and one way of describing him is as being like a wind. St John said this about the Holy Spirit: 'The wind blows wherever it pleases; you hear the sound it makes, but you cannot tell where it comes from or where it is going. So it is with the Spirit of God.' *(cf John 3:8)*

Why did Jesus send the Holy Spirit?

Through the Holy Spirit, Jesus remained with the apostles, and he remains with us in the same way today. God sent his Spirit to the apostles to begin the teaching of the Gospel throughout the world. The apostles knew that all the power and strength of their work lay in Jesus. They were useless without him and could not carry on with his work. Through the Holy Spirit he remained with them and his work could continue.

The word 'Spiritus' means breath or wind and that is how we often describe God's Spirit.

If someone asked you to describe the wind, what would you tell them?

- it cannot be seen, but we can see what it does, by making things move, trees bending and leaves blowing around
- we can feel it as it blows against our skin
- it can be very gentle or very powerful

We cannot see the Spirit himself but we can see what he does through the lives of people around us who allow him to guide their words and actions.

If you blew all of the air out of your body and did not breathe any more in, what would happen?

Without breathing you cannot live. The Spirit is the breath of God, who fills us with life and makes us strong.

Activity

Help each child to make a windmill to remind them that wind is one of the forms which the Spirit can take.

Closing Prayer

Come Holy Spirit,
and breathe your life into us,
so that we can bring Christ into the world
and touch the lives of others with his love.

WINDMILL.

1.

Two squares of differently coloured paper.

2.

Stick the two sheets together.

3.

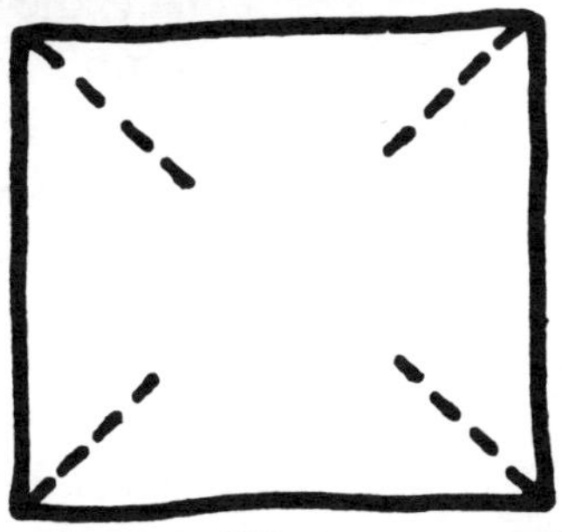

Fold the paper diagonally and cut along the creases halfway to the centre.

4.

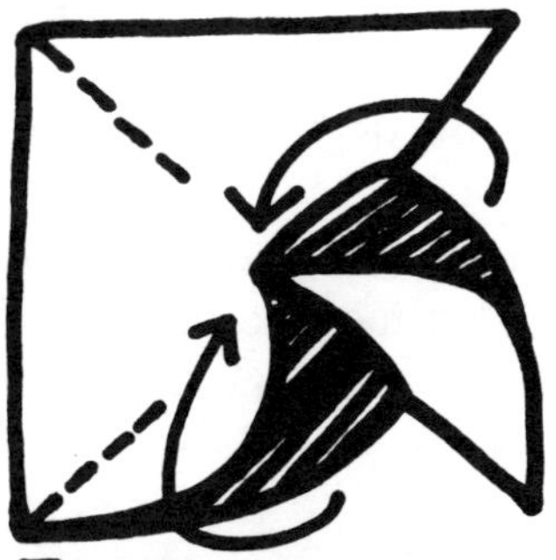

Fold every other point into the middle of the square and glue.

5.

Push a butterfly pin through the middle and through a straw.

6.

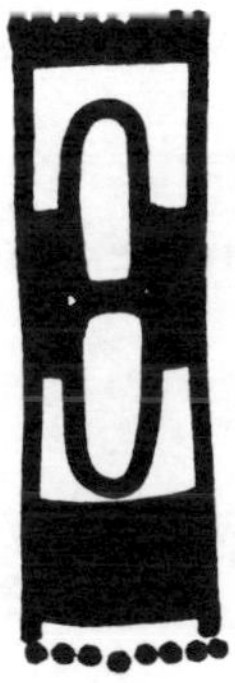

Open butterfly pin at back of straw.

Blow to make windmill turn.

7.

Jesus before Pontius Pilate

Reading

(cf John 18:33-37)

They brought Jesus before Pontius Pilate who asked him, 'Are you the king of the Jews?'

Jesus answered, 'My kingdom is not of this world.'

'So you do indeed claim to be a king!' said Pilate.

'You are the one who calls me king,' answered Jesus. 'I came into this world to share truth and love, and those who know and love the truth will listen to me.'

Discussion

Who was Pontius Pilate?

Pontius Pilate was the Roman governor of Judaea. He was in charge of the Roman army and responsible for keeping the peace. He acted as judge when serious crimes were committed.

Why was Jesus brought before Pontius Pilate?

The Jewish leaders had seen the welcome given to Jesus as he entered Jerusalem, and they were afraid of his position and power. They wanted to get rid of Jesus by whatever means they could, so they took Jesus to Pilate and asked for him to be sentenced to death.

What question did Pontius Pilate ask Jesus?

Jesus tried to explain that he was not a king who belonged to this world, but that he had come into the world to share his kingdom of love and goodness.

Did Pilate listen to Jesus and understand what he had said?

Pilate knew that Jesus was harmless and had done nothing wrong, but he was more interested in keeping the peace and not upsetting the Jewish leaders, than in seeing that justice was done. He allowed the Jewish leaders to have their own way, and eventually handed Jesus over to be put to death.

What happened after Jesus had suffered and died on the cross?

Three days later, on Easter Sunday, he rose from the dead and showed the world that he is the king of the universe, with the power to conquer death and bring new and everlasting life.

Activity

Cut out crown shapes from card and write on each one 'Christ is our King'. Decorate these and staple the crowns so that they can be worn or carried by the children.

Closing Prayer

God our Father
we thank you
for sending your only Son to be our saviour.
Help us to know and love your truth
and to listen to you always.

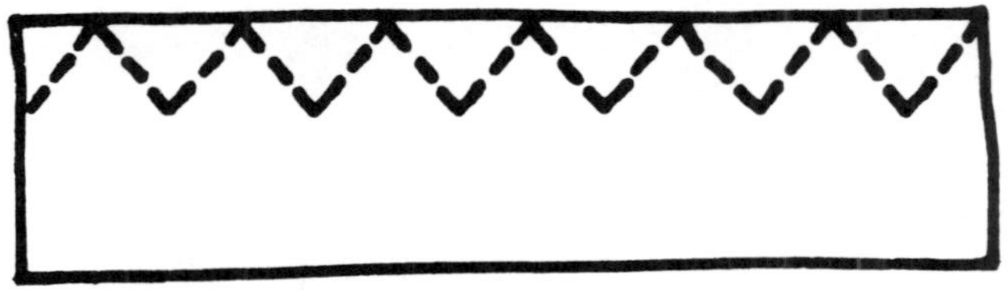
1. Cut out crown shapes from stiff card.

2. Decorate with stick-on-shapes and glitter.

3. Staple crowns two ends together.

4.

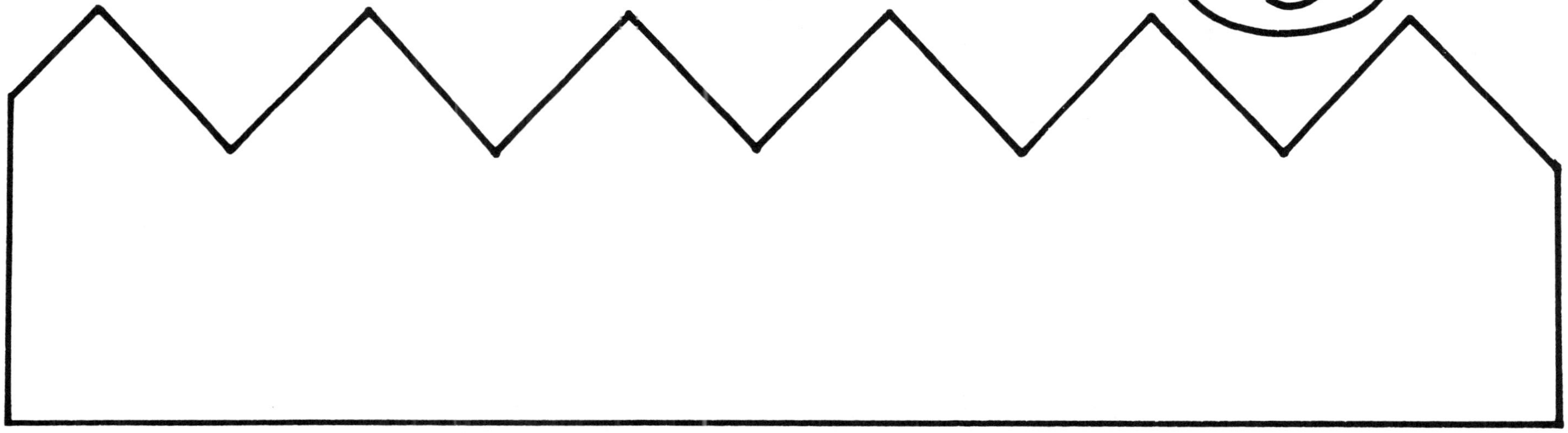

Jesus is alive. Alleluia! Alleluia!

Listening

(cf John 20:1-9)

Before sunrise on the Sunday morning, Mary of Magdala went to the tomb. As she got to the entrance, she saw that the stone had been rolled away and that the tomb was empty. She ran to the disciples saying, 'They have taken the Lord from the tomb and we don't know where they have put him!' Peter and another disciple, John, ran to the tomb and found it just as Mary had described, with the linen burial cloths lying on the ground. Peter went into the tomb first, followed by John. Until this moment they had not understood the Scriptures which had said, 'He must rise from the dead.' But now they saw, and they believed.

Talking

Why did Mary return to the tomb on Sunday morning?

Jesus had died late on Friday afternoon and the women had begun to prepare his body for burial using spices and ointments, as was their custom. The Jewish sabbath began at sunset on the Friday evening and work was not allowed on the sabbath, so they had to wait until the Sunday to complete their task.

What did Mary find when she arrived at the tomb?

Whom did she tell?

As the disciples ran to the tomb, can you imagine what they must have been thinking?

- had someone taken the Lord's body away?
- where had they put him?
- what could have happened?

Peter and John had raced to the tomb and found it empty. They could hardly believe that Jesus might be alive, but at that moment they began to hope that something as wonderful as this really could happen.

On Easter Day, we praise God that Jesus has destroyed death and is alive.

What do we give to each other on Easter Sunday as symbols of new life?

Easter eggs! Just as the chick in an egg must break free from its shell to begin a new life, so too, Jesus had to break free from death in the tomb. He had the new life which God has promised to us all!

Doing

Help the children to make this Easter greeting card.

Praying

Jesus, we thank you
for the joy of the resurrection,
when you rose from the dead
and were filled with new life.
Help us to remember that you suffered
and died on the cross for us,
so that we might share with you
the joy of everlasting life.

Jesus is Alive
Alleluia! Alleluia!

Doubting Thomas

Reading

(cf John 20:19-29)

On the Sunday after Jesus had died, his disciples sat huddled together in a locked room, hidden away for fear of being arrested. Suddenly Jesus appeared in the room with them. 'Peace be with you,' he said and he showed them the wounds in his hands and his side. His disciples were overjoyed to see their master again. 'As my father sent me, so I am sending you,' he said. Then breathing on them he said, 'Receive the Holy Spirit, and know that whoever you forgive, I will forgive also!'

The disciple called Thomas was not with the others when Jesus had appeared, and because he had not seen him with his own eyes, he did not believe that Jesus was alive.

A week later Jesus appeared to them again and, greeted them with the words, 'Peace be with you.' He showed his wounds to Thomas and said, 'Doubt no longer, Thomas.' At once Thomas fell to his knees and cried, 'My Lord and my God.'

Jesus said to him, 'You believe because you have seen me with your own eyes. Blessed are those who have not seen and yet believe.'

Discussion

When Jesus first appeared to the disciples in the locked room, which one of them was missing?

Thomas was not with the other disciples, and the Gospel does not explain where he was.

What did Jesus do when he appeared?

He shared the gift of his peace saying the words, 'Peace be with you'. Then he gave them the gift of the Holy Spirit to increase their faith and courage.

Did Thomas believe the disciples when they told him that Jesus had risen from the dead?

Thomas could not believe without seeing.

When Jesus appeared again he showed Thomas his wounds. Was he angry because Thomas had doubted?

Because Thomas could see and touch Jesus, he believed that he had risen from the dead. Jesus understood that many like Thomas would hear the story of the resurrection and be filled with doubt.

Can we 'see' the risen Jesus today?

Jesus lives amongst us and we can recognise his presence in the people around us. A kind action or a loving remark are signs of Christ's power working through other people.

What words did Thomas say when he recognised Jesus as the risen Lord?

'My Lord and my God'.

We cannot see Jesus but we *believe* that he is alive and present with us.

Activity

Cut out the shape of a large cross from a piece of stiff card and either paint it black or cover it with black or dark paper. Prepare small squares of coloured tissue paper, to make 'flowers'. Stick some of these onto the cross, while older children string others together to make a garland to hang on the cross. The 'Resurrection cross' can be attached to a stand or hung as a mobile. Add the caption: 'We believe Jesus is risen'.

Closing Prayer

Today we pray for those like Thomas,
who cannot believe without seeing.
Increase their faith Lord,
and help them to recognise you
in the people they meet every day.

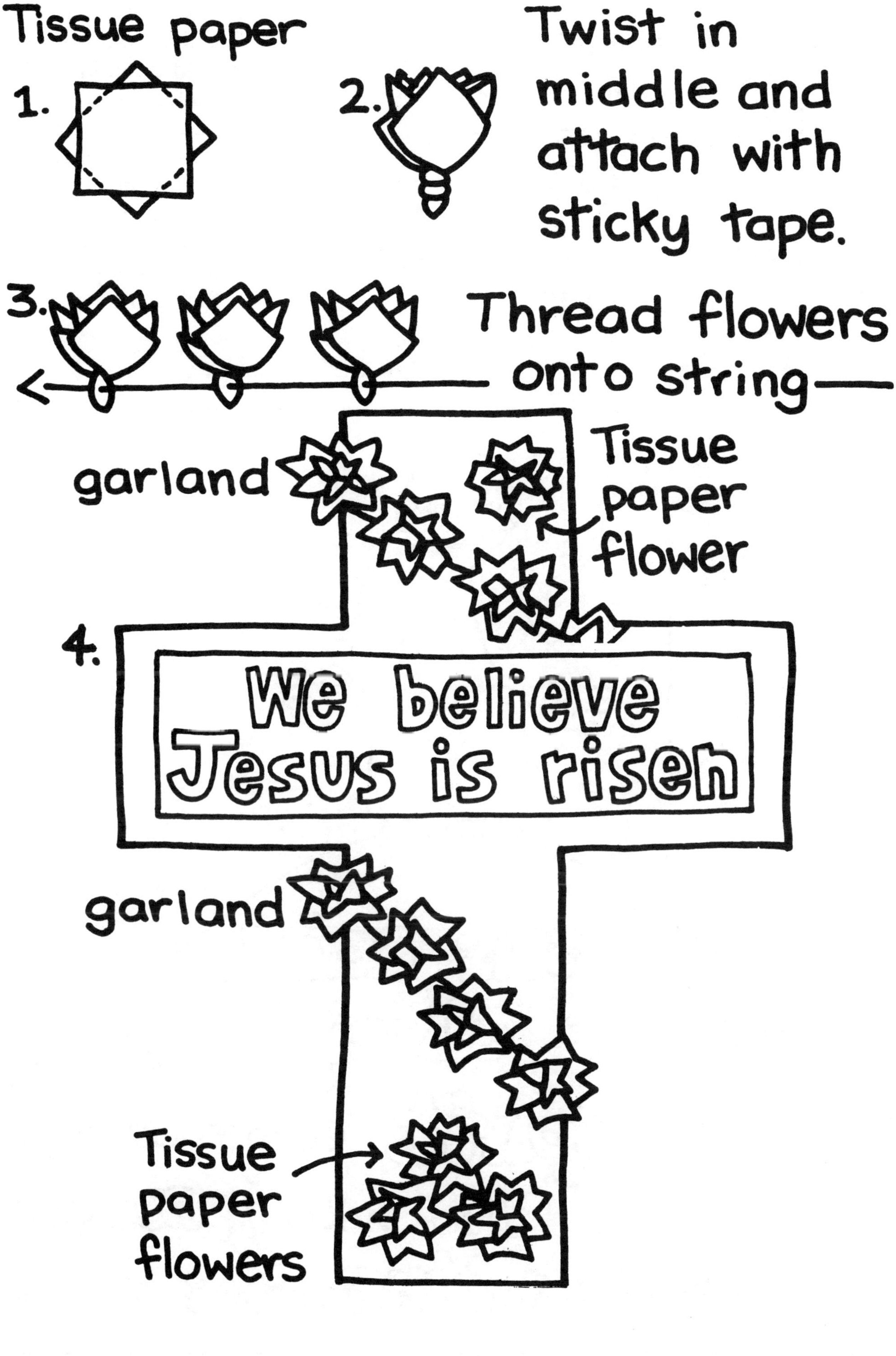
Tissue paper
1.
2.
Twist in middle and attach with sticky tape.
3.
Thread flowers onto string
4.
garland
Tissue paper flower
We believe Jesus is risen
garland
Tissue paper flowers

1. Photocopy onto thin card.
2. Colour and cut out.
3. Fold cloud inwards on dotted line _ . _ . _ .
4. Glue back of cloud **beyond** dotted line **only**.
5. Stick in position marked on main picture.
6. Fold cloud down to see Jesus disappear from their sight.

1. Photocopy onto thin card.
2. Colour flame and lettering and cut round outline.
3. Cut another long strip of card – the same width as the strip on the base of flame.
4. Staple or glue the right length of this to ends AB and CD so that the circle fits your head.
5. Wear your Holy Spirit flame!

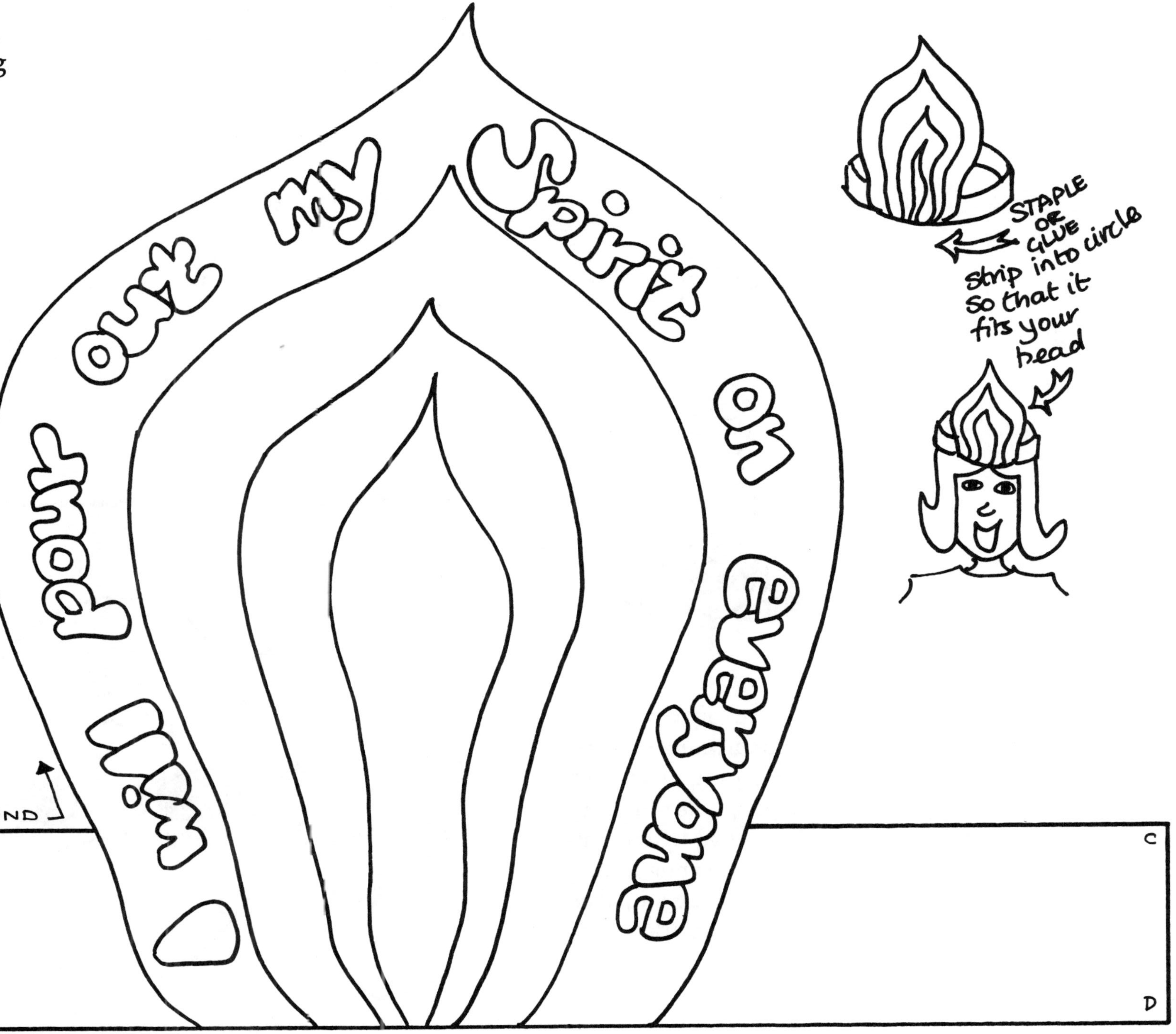

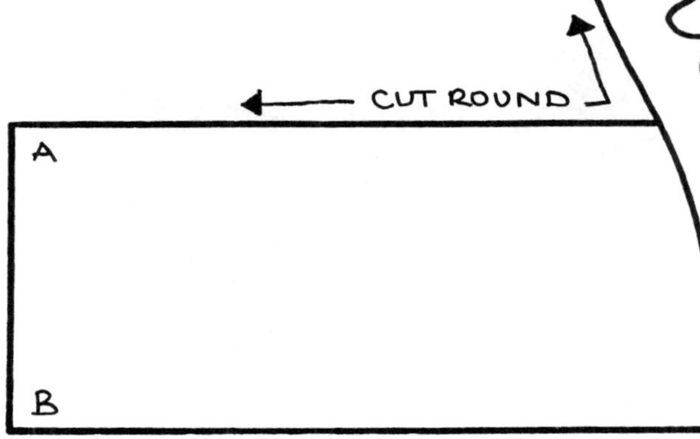

1. Photocopy this page onto thin card and page two onto paper.
2. Colour and cut out.
3. Cut man in half along thick line at middle.
4. Take zig-zag folded strip of paper from page two and glue top to head and bottom to legs of lame man.
5. Hang up lame man by piece of shirring elastic from top of head.

GLUE TO BODY

Peter said:

"In the name of

Jesus Christ

of Nazareth

I order you to

get up and walk!"

The man went

walking

and jumping

and praising God.

GLUE TO LEGS

1. Photocopy onto **paper**.
2. Cut out.
3. Zig-zag fold the strip, outwards on – – – lines and inwards on – · – · – lines.

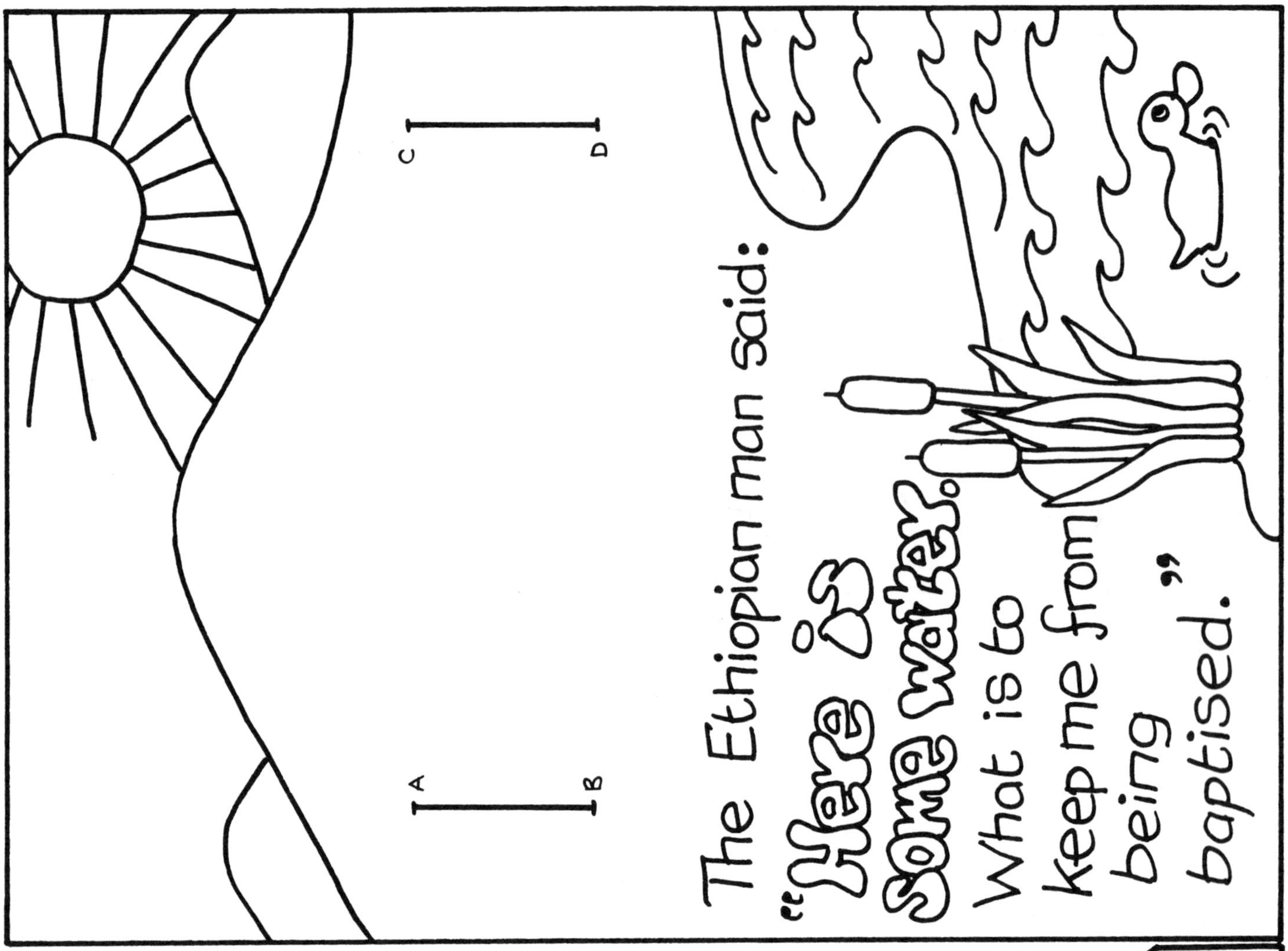

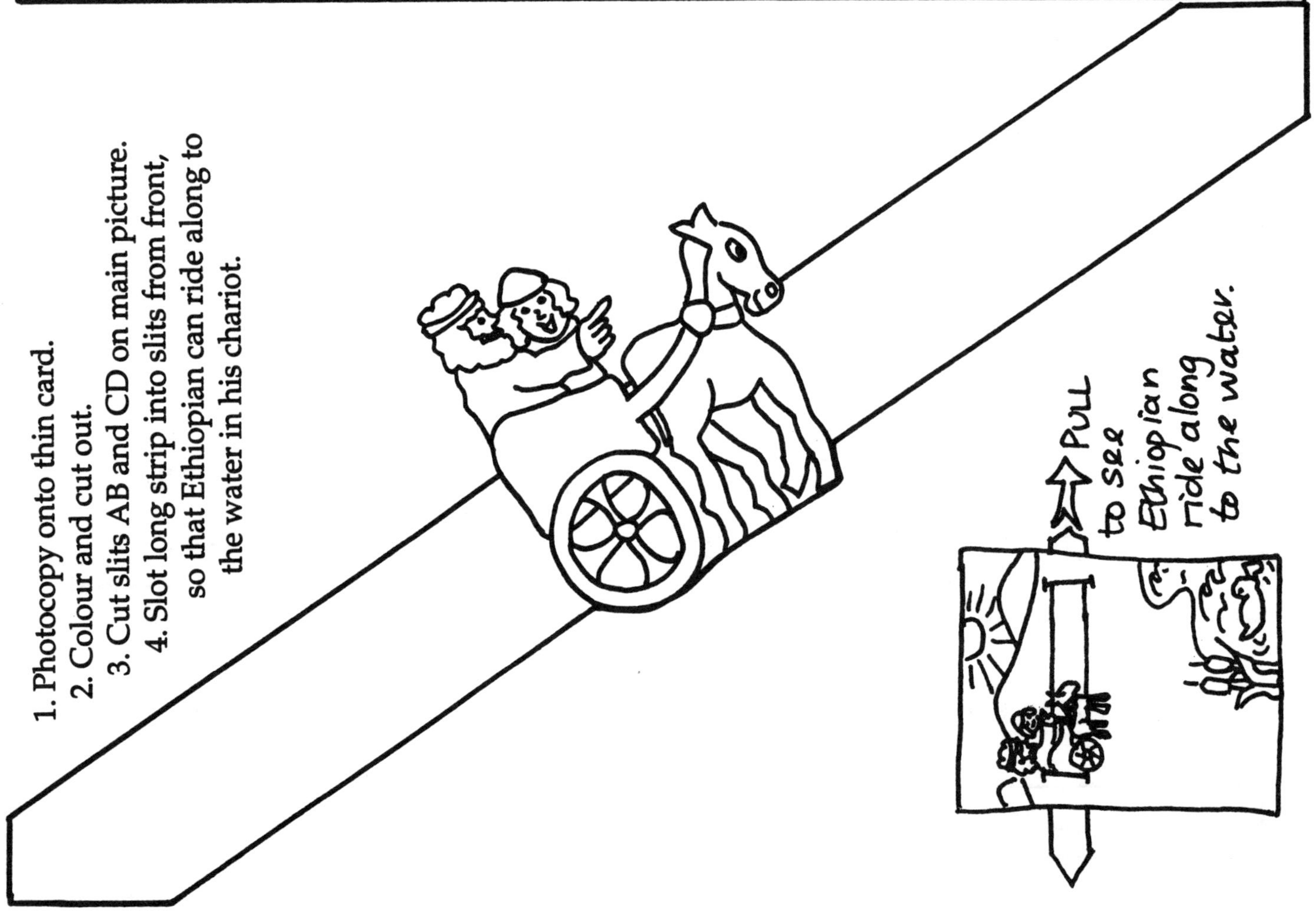

1. Photocopy onto thin card.
2. Colour and cut out.
3. Cut slits AB and CD on main picture.
4. Slot long strip into slits from front, so that Ethiopian can ride along to the water in his chariot.

1. Photocopy onto thin card.
2. Cut out around rectangle and cut off strip with Eutychus, along line XY.
3. Colour in.
4. Pierce dots A and B.
5. Cut along **curved** slits PQ and RS.
6. Slot strip XY from back through RS and PQ, so that Eutychus can be seen on main picture.
7. Attach with a paper fastener through A then B.
8. Move strip to see Eutychus fall out of window.

1. Photocopy onto thin card. 2. Colour and cut out.
3. Cut off strip with ship along line AB. 4. Cut slits XY and VW, slot ends of strip AB into these.
5. Fold inwards on dotted line _ . _ . _

6. Draw stormy sea on front of folded up piece.

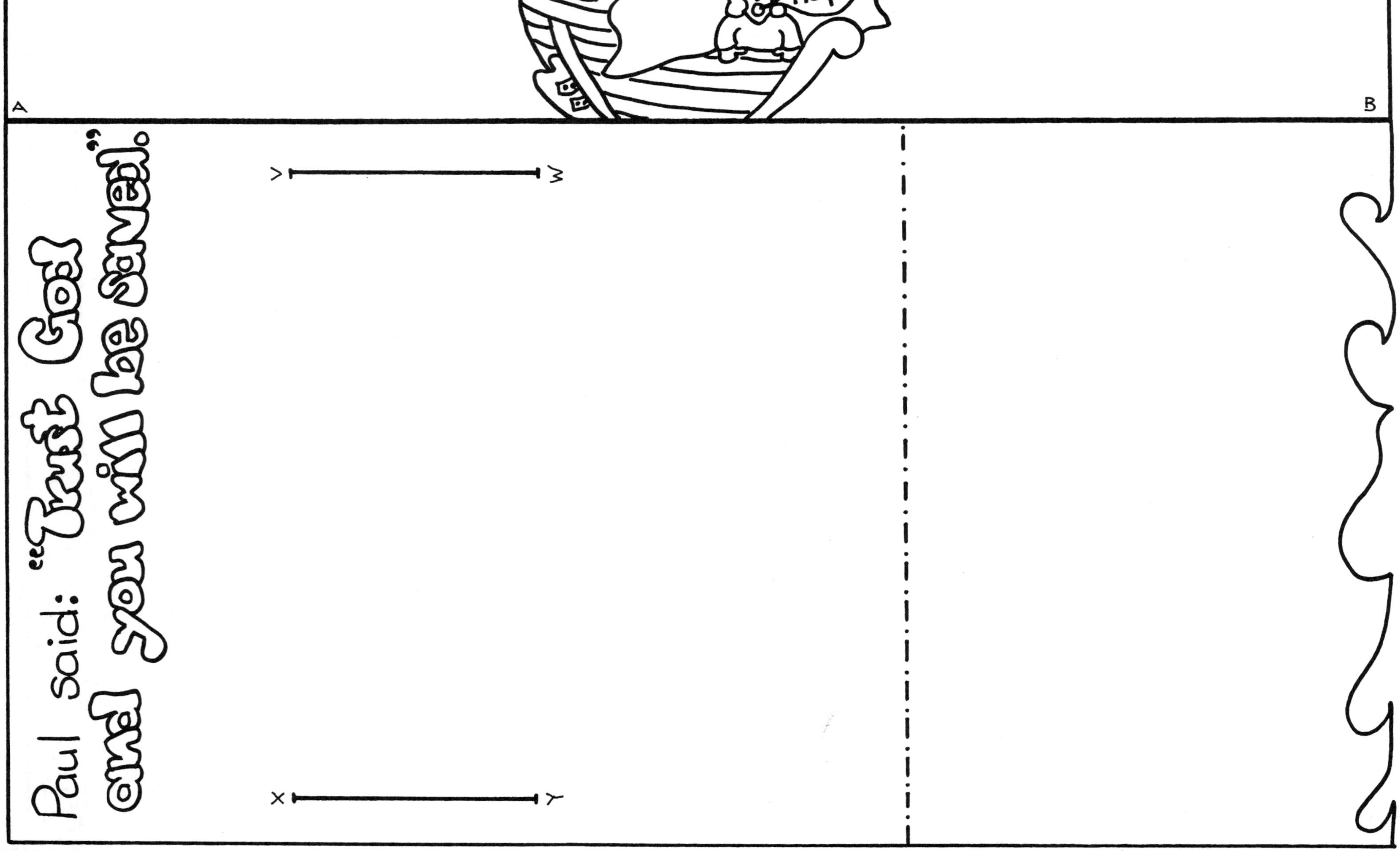